Mathematics Olympiad

Highly useful for all school students participating
in Various Olympiads & Competitions

Series Editor Keshav Mohan

Author Sanmeen Kaur

Class
5

arihant

ARIHANT PRAKASHAN, MEERUT

ARIHANT PRAKASHAN, MEERUT
All Rights Reserved

ॐ **Administrative & Production Offices**

Corporate Office 'Ramchhaya' 4577/15, Agarwal Road, Darya Ganj New Delhi -110002
Tele: 011- 47630600, 43518550; Fax: 011- 23280316

Head Office Kalindi, TP Nagar, Meerut (UP) - 250002
Tele: 0121-2401479, 2512970, 4004199; Fax: 0121-2401648

All disputes subject to Meerut (UP) jurisdiction only.

ॐ **Sales & Support Offices**

Agra, Ahmedabad, Bengaluru, Bhubaneswar, Bareilly, Chennai, Delhi, Guwahati, Haldwani, Hyderabad, Jaipur, Jalandhar, Jhansi, Kolkata, Kota, Lucknow, Meerut, Nagpur & Pune

ॐ **ISBN** 978-93-5251-206-5

ॐ **Price** ₹65

Typeset by Arihant DTP Unit at Meerut
Printed & Bound by Arihant Publications (I) Ltd. (Press Unit)

Production Team

Publishing Manager	Mahendra Singh Rawat	Page Layouting	Vijay Saini
Project Head	Mona Yadav	DTP Operator	Deepak kumar
Project Coordinator	Himanshu Verma	Cover Designer	Syed Darin Zaidi
Proof Reader	Kinshu Sharma	Inner Designer	Deepak Kumar

For further information about the products from Arihant
log on to www.arihantbooks.com or email to info@arihantbooks.com

Preface

Mathematics Olympiad Series for Class 2nd-10th is a series of books which will challenge the young inquisitive minds by the non-routine and exciting mathematical problems.

The main purpose of this series is to make the students ready for competitive exams. The school/board exams are of qualifying nature but not competitive, they do not help the students to prepare for competitive exams, which mainly have objective questions.

- **Need of Olympiad Series**
  This series will fill this gap between the school/board and competitive exams as this series have all questions in Objective format. This series helps students who are willing to sharpen their problem solving skills. Unlike typical assessment books, which emphasis on drilling practice, the focus of this series is on practicing problem solving techniques.

- **Development of Logical Approach**
  The thought provoking questions given in this series will help students to attain a deeper understanding of the concepts and through which students will be able to impart Reasoning/Logical/Analytical skills in them.

- **Complement Your School Studies**
  This series complements the additional preparation needs of students for regular school/board exams. Along with, it will also address all the requirements of the students who are approaching National/State level Olympiads.

I shall welcome criticism from the students, teachers, educators and parents. I shall also like to hear from all of you about errors and deficiencies, which may have remained in this edition and the suggestions for the next edition.

Editor

Contents

Number System

Indian Number System

Place value chart for 9-digit number

Crore		Lakh		Thousand		Ones			Period ←
Ten crore	Crore	Ten lakh	Lakh	Ten thousand	Thousand	Hundred	Tens	Ones	Place ←

International Number System

Place value chart for 12-digit number

Billion			Million			Thousand			Ones			Period ←
Hundred billion	Ten billion	Billion	Hundred million	Ten million	Million	Hundred thousand	Ten thousand	Thousand	Hundred	Tens	Unit/ones	Place ←

Rounding number to nearest thousand If the digit next to the digit in consideration is less than 5, then make the digits to the right of the digit in consideration '0' whereas, if the digit is greater than or equal to 5, then also add 1 to the digit in consideration.

e.g.   7643

Here,   6 > 5

So, 7643 will be rounded off to 8000 (i.e. 7 + 1).

Rounding number to nearest ten thousand If the digit next to the digit in consideration is less than 5, then make the digits to the right of the digit in consideration '0' whereas, if it is greater than or equal to 5, then also add 1 to the digit in consideration.

e.g. 42461

Here, 2 < 5, then 42461 will be rounded off to 40000.

Roman numeral system It is a system to represent mathematical numbers into combination of letters from latin alphabets.

e.g.

Mathematical number	1	2	3	4	5	6	7	8	9	10
Roman numerals	i	ii	iii	iv	v	vi	vii	viii	ix	x

Some other roman numerals representation are as follow :

L	C	D	M
50	100	500	1000

Let's Practice

1. Ms. Ben wrote four numbers on the board and asked the student to relate them according to the last lesson taught on number system. Which number she wrote is different from others?

(a) 1 lakh   (b) 100 thousand

(c) 1000 hundred   (d) 10 lakh

2. The area of Maharashtra is 8725651 sq km. Which system of numeration is used in the representation of the area of Maharashtra?

(a) International system

(b) Indian system

(c) Roman system

(d) None of the above

3. The Jim Corbett National Park has an area of approximately 1217403 acre. This number in expanded form written as

(a) 12 lakh 17 thousand 4 hundred 3 ones

(b) 1 lakh 12 thousand 43 hundred

(c) 12 lakh 170 thousand 43 ones

(d) 120 thousand 40 tens 3 ones

4. While writing a number in expanded form a student missed a number as shown below :

$800000000 + 900000 + 10000 + 5000 + \underline{\hspace{1cm}} + 8 = 800915018$

What is the number which he missed?

(a) 18   (b) 100

(c) 10   (d) 1080

5. Jack wrote the expanded form of number in words without using addition sign as follows. Nineteen lakh nineteen thousand nineteen hundred and nineteen.

The correct number he has written as

(a) 1920919   (b) 19191919

(c) 19192119   (d) None of these

6. Ramia wrote four phone numbers in her diary but forgot to write the name of the respective persons. She could only remember that her friend's phone number had 8 in the thousand's place. Then, her friend's number is

(a) 469821   (b) 829824

(c) 578242   (d) 982431

7. The price of a bike is ₹ 192000 when rounded off to nearest 1000. Which of the following could be the exact price of the bike?

(a) 191400   (b) 191499

(c) 192499   (d) 192505

8. In the number 5792456 the digit 7 stands for

(a) 7 hundred thousand   (b) 7 thousand

(c) 7 ten thousand   (d) 70 lakh

9. Difference between the place value and face value of 9 in the number 1297625 is

(a) 9   (b) 99991

(c) 89991   (d) 90001

10. Which of the following options is incorrectly matched?
    (a) CCC – 300   (b) DC – 400
    (c) CM – 900   (d) CL – 150

11. A college students' union held a raffle to raise money for a musical concert. Amaira drew ticket number 392704, Samantha drew ticket number 396491, Barbara drew ticket number 392677 and Celia drew ticket number 396449. Whose ticket had the largest number?
    (a) Celia   (b) Samantha
    (c) Amaira   (d) Barbara

12. In a certain state 5261989 students were enrolled in various schools. Of these 1965233 were primary school students and 2006756 were high school students, the rest attended middle school. What is the number of students enrolled in middle school rounded off to nearest lakh?
    (a) 2000000   (b) 1300000
    (c) 1200000   (d) None of these

13. Jivin made this table to show the number of visitors at 4 different beaches during one year.

Beach visitors

Beach	Number of visitors
Alligator point	12982
Port bella	12173
St. Joe's island	13704
Tucker's sound	12499

Which beach has number of visitors equal to 13000 when rounded off to nearest thousand?
(a) Tucker's sound
(b) St. Joe's island
(c) Port bella
(d) Alligator point

14. Choose the statement which is correct from the following given statements.
    (a) 99999999 is the successor of 100000000
    (b) The difference between the successor and predecessor of a number is 2
    (c) '0' is the smallest one-digit number
    (d) Face value and place value of a number are always same

15. While noting down the code number of a train from online railway site Maria wrote 14380502. How will she recite it to her brother correctly?
    (a) One four three eighty thousand five hundred two
    (b) One hundred forty three million eight thousand five hundred two
    (c) One crore forty three lakh eighty thousand five hundred two
    (d) Fourteen lakh thirty eight thousand five hundred two

16. On comparing the numbers, the signs that will come in the given boxes are
    I. 99999 ☐ 100000
    II. 9909409 ☐ 9990409
    III. 30100100 ☐ 30100099

	I	II	III			I	II	III
(a)	>	<	=		(b)	<	<	>
(c)	=	>	>		(d)	>	>	<

17. Fill in the blanks.

(i) digit	(ii) 10
(iii) 0	(iv) period
(v) 100	(vi) CCC
(vii) MMM	(viii) XXX

    I. Commas are inserted in a number after each _____ .
    II. Place value of a digit becomes _____ times as it moves from ten's place to thousand's place.
    III. There is no roman numeral to represent _____ .
    IV. 100 + 100 + 100 in roman numerals is _____ .

	I	II	III	IV
(a)	(iv)	(v)	(iii)	(vi)
(b)	(v)	(iv)	(iii)	(vii)
(c)	(i)	(v)	(ii)	(vii)
(d)	(i)	(ii)	(vii)	(viii)

18. Using all the digits given below, form the greatest possible 7-digit even number using all the digits where repetition of digit is allowed.
    | 7 | 4 | 0 | 5 |
    (a) 7540000   (b) 7775540
    (c) 7755440   (d) 7777540

19. 42040 + ____ is 10100 less than smallest 6-digit number. Then, the missing number is

(a) 32190　　　　(b) 47860

(c) 46060　　　　(d) 52440

20. Match the following columns and choose the correct option.

Column A		Column B	
I.	V + V	(i)	6
II.	XXXIV – XXVIII	(ii)	9
III.	LI – XL	(iii)	10
IV.	XCIX – XC	(iv)	11

```
        I     II    III   IV
(a)    (i)   (ii)  (iii) (iv)
(b)    (iii) (i)   (iv)  (ii)
(c)    (iv)  (iii) (i)   (ii)
(d)    (iii) (i)   (ii)  (iv)
```

21. A cricket stadium manager counted the number of matches held in each month.

Matches held

Months	Number of matches
March	XCVI
April	LXXXV
May	XCIX
June	XCV

In which month the stadium had the lowest number of matches?

(a) March　　(b) April　　(c) May　　(d) June

22. In the given abacus where should a ring (one) be added, so as to make the number lying between 24631 and 25212?

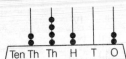

(a) One　　　　　　(b) Hundred

(c) Thousand　　　(d) Ten thousand

23. The smallest correctly formed roman number using each numeral once from the roman numerals I, V, X, L, C, D and M is

(a) MDCLXVI

(b) MCDXLIV

(c) MCDXLVI

(d) Cannot be determined

24. State 'T' for true and 'F' for false and mark the correct option.

I. Place value and face value are always equal for '0'.

II. Successor of a number is one less than the number.

III. Predecessor of the smallest natural number is the smallest even number.

IV. The roman numeral to represent V – I = IV

```
        I    II   III  IV          I    II   III  IV
(a) T    T    F    T    (b) F    T    T    F
(c) T    F    F    T    (d) F    F    T    F
```

25. What least number should be added to 3543467 such that place value of 1 in the resulting numeral becomes 100000000?

(a) 70000000　　　(b) 96456533

(c) 95634671　　　(d) 95465633

Direction (Q. Nos. 26-27) Use the table given below to answer the following questions.

Number of students participated in FBD's Olympiad

National FBD Science Olympiad	5748129
National FBD Maths Olympiad	6275492
National FBD English Olympiad	6275501

26. Number of students who participated in National FBD English Olympiad to nearest ten thousand is

(a) 6200000　　　(b) 6280000

(c) 6000000　　　(d) 6285000

27. In which Olympiad the digit 5 is at one lakh place?

(a) National FBD Maths Olympiad

(b) National FBD Science Olympiad

(c) National FBD English Olympiad

(d) None of the above

28. Ms. Hendrick's 5th grade class collected 2803 waste papers to recycle in one month and 3745 waste papers the next month. She estimated the total number of papers for both months by adding 3000 and 4000. Would her estimate be more or less than the actual answer?

(a) Less, because she rounded both numbers up

(b) More, because she rounded both numbers up

(c) Less, because she rounded both numbers down

(d) More, because she rounded both numbers down

Operations on Numbers

The four basic mathematical operations are

- ✦ Addition   ✦ Subtraction   ✦ Multiplication   ✦ Division

Addition   Adding two (or more) numbers means to find their sum.

The numbers that we add are called addends.

Subtraction   Subtracting one number from another number means to find the difference between them.

The greater number in subtraction is called minuend.

The smaller number which is being subtracted is called subtrahend.

Multiplication   It is defined as to calculate the result of repeated additions of two numbers. e.g. $2 \times (6) = 12$ i.e. $6 + 6$

We have, Multiplicand $\times$ Multiplier $=$ Product

Division   It is the method to find out how many times one number is contained in another. e.g. $6 \div 2 = 3$ i.e. $6 - 2 = 4 - 2 = 2 - 2 = 0, 3$ times.

We have, Dividend $=$ Divisor $\times$ Quotient $+$ Remainder

Order of operations   It refers to the rule used to classify which operation should be performed first in a given mathematical expression.

Rules for Order of Operations

- ✦ Solve things in brackets first
- ✦ Divide (working from left to right)
- ✦ Multiply
- ✦ Add
- ✦ Subtract

Do first	**B** Brackets	(),{},[]
	O Of	
	D Division	/, ÷
	M Multiplication	×
	A Addition	+
Do last	**S** Subtraction	−

Let's Practice

1. From the following numbers

   277, 316, 479, 582

   Choose the correct option that fill in the blanks to complete the following operation.

   _____ – _____ =305

   (a) 479, 277   (b) 582, 277

   (c) 582, 316   (d) 479, 316

2. Maria asked her younger sister to pick a calculator which is not showing the correct calculation and give it for repair. Which of the calculator will her younger sister choose, if the calculator screen shows the given numbers?

   (a) [45789 × 1=45789]   (b) [4579 × 0 = 0]

   (c) [45789×10=10]   (d) [45789–0=45789]

3. Manisha bought four cupcakes that all cost the same amount. Which operation she must use to find the total cost of them, if cost of one cupcake is ₹ 10?

   (a) Subtracting 10 from 4
   (b) Adding 10 to 4
   (c) Multiplying 10 by 4
   (d) Dividing 10 by 4

4. If each letter represents a different number, then the number represented by ABCDE in the following operation is

   $$
   \begin{array}{r}
   A\,B\,C\,D\,E \\
   \times\ 4 \\
   \hline
   1\,2\,3\,4\,5\,6
   \end{array}
   $$

	A	B	C	D	E
(a)	3	0	8	6	4
(b)	3	1	8	3	9
(c)	1	2	3	4	5
(d)	5	4	3	2	1

5. A football team sold 215 youth tickets for ₹ 4 each and 467 adult tickets for ₹ 9 each. Which expression can be used to find how much more money the football team made on adult tickets than on youth tickets?

   (a) (215×4) – (467×9)   (b) (215×9) – (467×4)
   (c) (467×9) – (215×4)   (d) (467×4) – (215×9)

6. Which number will come in the start box to have a meaningful proceeding?

   (a) 360
   (b) 384
   (c) 1350
   (d) 1.50

   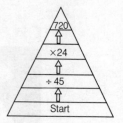

7. Complete the product of 17 and 56 using the box method given below and fill in the missing mumber.

   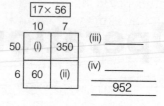

	(i)	(ii)	(iii)	(iv)
(a)	50	40	500	130
(b)	500	42	850	102
(c)	600	35	420	110
(d)	160	30	410	56

8. A car route is 9 km long. The car goes through the route 2 times each day. How many kilometres will the car drive in 5 days?

   (a) 100 km   (b) 50 km
   (c) 10 km   (d) 90 km

9. Benjamin earns ₹ 1840 in a week. How much money will he earn in 3 months 3 weeks, if every month has 4 weeks?

   (a) ₹ 12200
   (b) ₹ 27000
   (c) ₹ 19900
   (d) ₹ 27600

10. Use the numbers in the box given below to complete the passage and choose the correct option.

495	33	396	55

    Four friends decided to visit the city nearby during their vacations by car. They left home at 7 am and travelled about

(i) _____ km in 9 hours, that is an average of

(ii) _____ km per hour.

      (i)   (ii)

(a) 495 33

(b) 495 55

(c) 396 33

(d) 396 55

11. 2961 sweets were given to the children in an orphanage. Each child received 3 sweets. How many children were there?

(a) 8883   (b) 987

(c) 2964   (d) 2958

12. Four students in Ms. Banerjee's class simplify the expression below :

$$7 + 21 \div 3 - 8 \times 2 + 9$$

The first step of each of the four students is shown in the table below :

Students	First step
Megha	$7 + 21$
Jasmin	$3 - 8$
Sanchi	$21 \div 3$
Kruti	$2 + 9$

Which student performs a first step that is correct?

(a) Megha   (b) Jasmin

(c) Sanchi   (d) Kruti

13. Match the following columns and choose the correct option.

Column A		Column B	
I.	Minuend − Subtrahend	(i)	Sum
II.	Addend + Addend	(ii)	Product
III.	Multiplicand × Multiplier	(iii)	Quotient
IV.	Dividend ÷ Divisor	(iv)	Difference

      I   II   III   IV

(a) (i) (ii) (iii) (iv)

(b) (iv) (iii) (ii) (i)

(c) (iii) (iv) (i) (ii)

(d) (iv) (i) (ii) (iii)

14. What number is it?

    I. It is a two-digit number.

    II. Its unit digit is 1 subtracted from $2 \times (2 \div 2)$.

    III. Its ten's digit is 15 subtracted from 36 and then divided by 7.

(a) 42   (b) 13

(c) 81   (d) 31

15. A number in the form 'pqrspqrs' when divided by pqrs gives

(a) 11   (b) 1001

(c) 10001   (d) Cannot be determined

16. If A, B and C are natural numbers and A = 76240 and B = 3245. If the sum of A and B is equal to the difference of C and B, then the possible value of C is

(a) 82730   (b) 72995

(c) 79485   (d) Cannot be determined

17. Fill in the blanks using the appropriate options from the box given.

(i) 47		(ii) XXVII	
(iii) 3		(iv) $100 + 20$	
(v) 9		(vi) XXXV	
(vii) 100×20		(viii) $100 \div 20$	
(ix) units and tens		(x) tens and hundred	
(xi) units, tens and hundred			

    I. A number is divisible by 9, if the sum of the digits of the number is divisible by _____ .

    II. XI + XVI + XX = _____

    III. If there are 100 toffees in a packet, then the number of toffees in 20 such bags is _____ .

    IV. A number is divisible by 8, if the number formed by the digits in _____ places is divisible by 8.

      I   II   III   IV

(a) (v) (vi) (viii) (x)

(b) (iii) (i) (iv) (ix)

(c) (v) (i) (vii) (xi)

(d) (iii) (vi) (viii) (x)

18. Which number, when placed in the box makes the following numbers sentence true?

$$18 - 6 \times 2 + 21 \div 3 = \square$$

(a) 9   (b) 12
(c) 13   (d) 15

19. In a city, age of 34768 people is below 20, age of 57498 people is between 20 and 30 and age of remaining people is above 30. If the total population of the village is 100000, then the number of people who are above 30, is

(a) 92266   (b) 42502
(c) 65232   (d) 7734

20. There are 15 rows of mango trees in a farm. Each row has 325 trees. Trees of 6 rows are cut down. The total number of remaining mango trees in the park is

(a) 2925   (b) 4875
(c) 1950   (d) None of these

21. State 'T' for true and 'F' for false and mark the correct option.

I. When any number is divisible by 1, the quotient is 1 only.

II. Number divisible by 10 must have zero as a unit digit.

III. $(4 \times 6) + (4 \times 10) = 4 \times (6 + 10)$

IV. The greatest number in the subtraction is called minuend.

	I	II	III	IV		I	II	III	IV
(a)	F	T	T	T	(b)	T	T	T	F
(c)	F	F	F	T	(d)	T	F	F	T

22. If

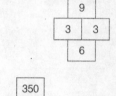

$$\triangle + \triangle + \square = 225$$
$$\triangle - \square = 30$$

Then, the value of $\triangle$ is
(a) 90   (b) 80
(c) 95   (d) 85

23. On the basis of the given block, find the missing numbers.

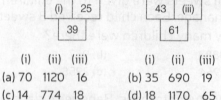

	(i)	(ii)	(iii)
(a)	70	1120	16
(b)	35	690	19
(c)	14	774	18
(d)	18	1170	65

Direction (Q. Nos. 24-25) The table below shows the number of food items collected by four classes for a donation camp. It also shows the number of days each class collects food items during the donation program.

Class	Packets of food items (per day)	Days collected
Class 1	728	25
Class 2	225	40
Class 3	374	20
Class 4	280	30

24. Which class collected the maximum number of food items?

(a) Class 1
(b) Class 2
(c) Class 3
(d) Class 4

25. If class 2 has to collect the same number of packets in 40 days as collected by class 1 in 25 days, then how many packets class 2 has to collect in one day?

(a) 728
(b) 210
(c) 455
(d) 242

Factors and Multiples

Factors The numbers which we multiply together to get another number are called factors of that number.

e.g.   2 and 3 are factors of 6.

Even numbers   The numbers which are divisible by 2 are called even numbers.

e.g.   2, 4, 6, 8, 10, 12, etc., all are even numbers.

Odd numbers   The numbers which are not divisible by 2 are called odd numbers.

e.g.   1, 3, 5, 7, 9, 11, etc., all are odd numbers.

Prime numbers   Numbers which have only two factors, i.e. 1 and the number itself.

e.g.   2, 3, 5 etc., all are prime numbers.

Twin primes   Two consecutive prime numbers whose difference is 2, are called twin primes.

e.g.   11 and 13 are twin primes.

Coprime numbers   Two numbers whose common factor is 1 are called coprime numbers.

e.g.   5 and 9 are coprime numbers.

Highest Common Factor (HCF)   The largest common factor of two or more numbers is called their HCF.

Multiple   These are the numbers which are the products of any given whole number and another whole number.

e.g.   6, 12, 18 and 24 are multiplies of 6.

Least Common Multiple (LCM)   The smallest among all the common factors of two or more numbers is called their LCM.

Let's Practice

1. The missing number in triangle II on the basis of the rule followed in triangle I is

(a) 10   (b) 15   (c) 25   (d) 30

2. In a Mathematics paper, score of three girls are as follow

Annie Lowest multiple of 10

Jass Fourth multiple of 3

Krish Highest factor of 15

Which of the following is correct about the score of the girls?

(a) Annie < Jass < Krish   (b) Jass < Annie < Krish

(c) Krish < Annie < Jass   (d) None of these

3.

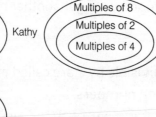

Who drew the correct picture?

(a) Jamaica   (b) Kathy   (c) Jimmy   (d) None of these

4. In the following figure, one of the figure is different from other, choose the odd one out.

(a)   (b)

(c)   (d)

5. Fill in the blanks using the given below box and choose the correct option.

(i) $\dfrac{LCM}{HCF}$	(ii) prime, composite
(iii) LCM − HCF	(iv) LCM × HCF
(v) coprimes	(vi) factor, multiple
(vii) twin prime	(viii) LCM + HCF

I. '1' is the only number which is neither _____ nor _____ .

II. Two consecutive prime numbers whose difference is 2 are called _____ .

III. Every number is a _____ and a _____ of itself.

IV. The LCM and HCF of two numbers is given, then product of the numbers is _____ .

	I	II	III	IV
(a)	(viii)	(v)	(ii)	(i)
(b)	(ii)	(vii)	(vi)	(iv)
(c)	(viii)	(vii)	(ii)	(iv)
(d)	(ii)	(v)	(vi)	(i)

6.

Which of the following options will have the result equal to the HCF of the above marked angles?

(a) LCM (2°, 5°)   (b) HCF (10°, 100°)

(c) Both (a) and (b)   (d) None of these

7. Saria intended to complete her three books in such a way that she reads Book *A* on every 4th day, Book *B* on every 5th day and Book *C* on every 6th day. On which day will she read all the three books together?

(a) 50th day   (b) 60th day

(c) 72nd day   (d) 64th day

8. In the following figure, both figures are follow similar relation. On the basis of their relations, the value of *x* is

(a) 5   (b) 4   (c) 6   (d) 24

9. After every nineth visit to a restaurant, Saran receives a free beverage. After every twelfth visit she receives a free appetiser. On which visit will she receive a free beverage and a free appetiser both?

(a) 12th   (b) 27th   (c) 36th   (d) 48th

10. Robin The greatest common factor of 75 and 225 is 75.

Robert 2 is the factor of every even number

Who said the correct statement?

(a) Robin   (b) Robert

(c) Both (a) and (b)   (d) None of these

11. Which of the following shows the correct factorisation of 90?

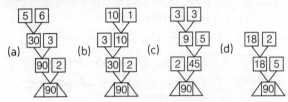

12. If the only factors of X are 2, 5, 6 and the only factors of Y are 4 and 8, then the smallest values of X and Y are

(a) 20, 30   (b) 30, 8   (c) 15, 25   (d) 23, 27

13. The following figure shows the factor tree of 150. On the basis of factor tree, fill the missing numbers and choose the correct option.

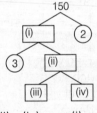

	(i)	(ii)	(iii)	(iv)		(i)	(ii)	(iii)	(iv)
(a)	25	15	3	5	(b)	75	25	5	5
(c)	50	10	2	3	(d)	148	72	16	4

14. Janelle is sending different contents on her daughter's hostel address. Following is the content list :

Content's for Janelle's daughter

Object	Weight
Pad of paper and a pencil	8 oz
Colouring books	16 oz
Dictionary	4 oz
Toy	14 oz

If these contents are to be packed separately in packets of same weight, then what would be the maximum weight of the packets having same weight?

(a) 4 oz   (b) 8 oz   (c) 7 oz   (d) 2 oz

15. A rectangular sheet of some perimeter is to be cut into smaller pieces of equal size. It can be cut out into three types of same sized sheets of the following sizes.

Perimeter 3 units ▭   Perimeter 4 units ▭   Perimeter 5 units ▭
I   II   III

What can be the least perimeter of the larger rectangular sheet from which above smaller sheets can be cut out?

(a) 40 units   (b) 45 units   (c) 50 units   (d) 60 units

16. Rosy and Luke are playing a game called "Guess my numbers."

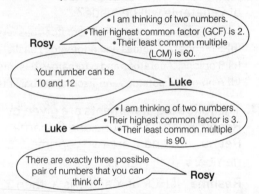

Who gave the correct answer to the others question?

(a) Rosy   (b) Luke

(c) Both (a) and (b)   (d) None of these

17. Match the following columns and choose the correct option.

Column A	Column B
I. Numbers which are not multiples of 2.	(i) Odd numbers
II. Numbers which have more than two factors.	(ii) Prime numbers
III. Successor of every odd number.	(iii) Composite numbers
IV. Numbers having only two factors, 1 and itself.	(iv) Even numbers

	I	II	III	IV		I	II	III	IV
(a)	(i)	(ii)	(iii)	(iv)	(b)	(iv)	(iii)	(ii)	(i)
(c)	(ii)	(i)	(iii)	(iv)	(d)	(i)	(iii)	(iv)	(ii)

18. Miranda counted to 60 using multiple of 6. Her friends concluded the following statements

Lara	Duke	Chrish	Jack
They all are odd numbers.	They all have 6 in the ones place.	They can all be divided evenly by 3.	They can all be divided by 12.

Who said the correct statement?

(a) Lara   (b) Duke   (c) Chrish   (d) Jack

Direction (Q. Nos. 19-20) A vegetable vendor wants to pack 56 onions, 32 potatoes and 64 tomatoes in a basket containing an equal number of vegetables of same type.

19. What is the maximum number of vegetables of same type in each basket can he keep?

(a) 10   (b) 8   (c) 7   (d) 12

20. How many number of baskets of each type of vegetable will be made?

(a) 7 onions, 4 potatoes and 8 tomatoes baskets
(b) 5 onions, 7 potatoes and 6 tomatoes baskets
(c) 8 onions, 3 potatoes and 6 tomatoes baskets
(d) 6 onions, 4 potatoes and 7 tomatoes baskets

21. The following statements are given by Reenu, Reshma, Karuna and Suparna.
Reenu If X and Y are two coprime numbers, their HCF is 1.

Reshma If HCF of X and Y is X, then Y is divisible by X.

Karuna If HCF of X and Y is equal to the HCF of Y and Z, HCF of X and Z is also the same.

Suparna If $X + 1 = Y$, X and Y are coprime numbers.

Who is not correct?

(a) Reenu   (b) Reshma
(c) Suparna   (d) Karuna

22. Margret joined three activities i.e. singing, dancing and drawing.

I. She went for singing class once in every 3 days.

II. She went for dancing class once in every 4 days.

III. She went for drawing class once in every 6 days.

The calendar below shows that Margret did all the activities on Monday 5th.

NOVEMBER

S	M	T	W	T	F	S
				1	2	3
4	5	6	7	8	9	10
11	12	13	14	15	16	17
18	19	20	21	22	23	24
25	26	27	28	29	30	

On which day will Margret again do all three activities on the same day?

(a) 12th, Monday   (b) 17th, Saturday
(c) 21st, Wednesday   (d) 30th, Friday

23. State 'T' for true and 'F' for false and choose the correct option.

I. '1' is a factor of every number.

II. '0' is neither prime nor composite.

III. LCM of two numbers = Product of number × HCF.

IV. HCF of two coprime numbers is 0.

	I	II	III	IV		I	II	III	IV
(a)	F	T	F	T	(b)	T	F	T	F
(c)	F	F	T	T	(d)	T	T	F	F

Direction (Q. No. 24) The prime factors of 80 and 110 are shown by the following rectangles. On the basis of it answer the following.

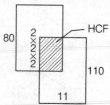

24. The common area between the two rectangles will have

(a) 2 × 5   (b) 5 × 11   (c) 2 × 5 × 11   (d) 11 × 2

25. In an amusement park, a fountain erects water, in different colours at different intervals of time. The water of colour red comes out at every 40 minutes, of colour blue comes out at every 50 minutes and of colour yellow comes out at every hour.

If the water of all the colours came out together at 8 am. At what time will they come out together again?

(a) 3 pm   (b) 12 noon   (c) 6 pm   (d) 8 pm

Fractions

When an object or a whole is divided into a number of equal parts, then each part is called a fraction. Fraction is further divided into following types.

Proper fraction   A fraction in which numerator is less than the denominator.

e.g. $\frac{2}{3}$ is a proper fraction.

Improper fraction   A fraction in which numerator is greater than or equal to the denominator.   e.g. $\frac{7}{3}$ is an improper fraction.

Mixed fraction   A fraction with a whole part and a fractional part.

e.g. $1\frac{2}{3}$ is a mixed fraction.

Like fractions   Fractions having same denominators are called like fractions.

e.g. $\frac{2}{7}$ and $\frac{4}{7}$ are like fractions.

Unlike fractions   Fractions having different denominators are called unlike fractions.

e.g. $\frac{3}{11}$ and $\frac{3}{13}$ are unlike fractions.

Equivalent fractions   Fractions that represent the same number, i.e. their simplest

form is same (or equal). e.g. $\frac{4}{5}$ and $\frac{16}{20}$ are equivalent fractions.

Reciprocal   The multiplicative inverse of a number/fraction is called its reciprocal. It is obtained by "turning the fraction over".

e.g. $\frac{2}{3}$ is the reciprocal of $\frac{3}{2}$.

Let's Practice

1. Greg ate the following part of the cake and left the remaining for his friends. What part of cake did Greg eat?

(a) $\dfrac{1}{2}$ (b) $\dfrac{3}{4}$

(c) $\dfrac{1}{4}$ (d) $\dfrac{2}{6}$

2. Tom talked on the telephone to three friends. He talked to Hary for $\dfrac{1}{6}$ hour, to Geet for $\dfrac{5}{3}$ hours and to Ryan for $\dfrac{1}{4}$ hour. How much time did Tom spend on the telephone?

(a) $3\dfrac{1}{6}$ hours   (b) $2\dfrac{1}{12}$ hours

(c) $4\dfrac{1}{6}$ hours   (d) $3\dfrac{1}{12}$ hours

3. While writing the answers to the questions given to Jeba in homework, she made a mistake in writing one of the answer in simplest form. Pick the answer she wrote incorrectly?

(a) $\dfrac{3}{15}$ (b) $\dfrac{16}{31}$

(c) $\dfrac{9}{17}$ (d) $\dfrac{4}{5}$

4. How many minimum unshaded rectangles should be added to make the figure $\dfrac{2}{3}$ part shaded?

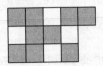

(a) 2   (b) 1

(c) 3   (d) 4

5. Pamela drew a picture using different shapes. What part of the picture has stars in it?

(a) $\dfrac{1}{2}$ (b) $\dfrac{1}{3}$ (c) $\dfrac{1}{4}$ (d) $\dfrac{2}{3}$

6. Florence forgot to colour some part of her art class assignment. If each whole part carries 1 mark, then how much marks did she get?

(a) $\dfrac{4}{5}$ (b) $4\dfrac{4}{7}$ (c) $4\dfrac{3}{7}$ (d) $\dfrac{1}{5}$

7. Which point on the number line represents $1\dfrac{9}{10}$?

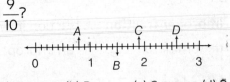

(a) A (b) B (c) C (d) D

8. Mario made some holes in a triangle as shown in the picture. Determine the fraction to represent the part of triangles having odd number of holes.

(a) $\dfrac{1}{3}$ (b) $\dfrac{4}{9}$ (c) $\dfrac{5}{9}$ (d) $\dfrac{2}{3}$

9. Eric had 12 weeks of summer vacation. He practiced guitar everyday and learned 6 new songs. How many songs did Eric learn each week?

(a) 2 songs   (b) 10 songs

(c) 5 songs   (d) $\dfrac{1}{2}$ of a song

10. Which of the situations given below can be represented by the fraction $\dfrac{8}{24}$?

(a) 8 friends share 24 pies equally. How much pie does each person get?

(b) Grimmy sleeps 8 hours each day (24 hours). What part of each day does Grimmy sleep?

(c) Mark uses 2 dozen bananas to make banana shakes for his 8 children. How many bananas are in each shake?

(d) 24 toys are distributed into 8 groups. How many toys are received by each group?

11.

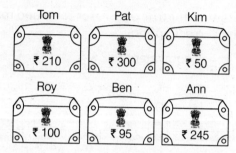

Tom ₹ 210 Pat ₹ 300 Kim ₹ 50
Roy ₹ 100 Ben ₹ 95 Ann ₹ 245

Six friends save money for an orphanage to donate on an occasion of children's day.

Find who saved $\dfrac{1}{20}$ th of the total amount saved by all the friends.

(a) Kim (b) Pat (c) Ben (d) Roy

12.

×	×	★	◇
×			□
○	○		□
○	○	★	□

× → Black
○ → Red
★ → Green
□ → Yellow
◇ → Blue

Above figure shows the different colours filled in the squares.

On the basis of it, match the following columns and choose the correct option.

Column A		Column B	
I.	Red	(i)	$\dfrac{1}{8}$
II.	Green	(ii)	$\dfrac{1}{16}$
III.	Blue	(iii)	$\dfrac{1}{4}$
IV.	Black	(iv)	$\dfrac{3}{16}$

	I	II	III	IV		I	II	III	IV
(a)	(i)	(iii)	(iii)	(iv)	(b)	(iii)	(i)	(ii)	(iv)
(c)	(iv)	(iii)	(ii)	(i)	(d)	(ii)	(i)	(iv)	(iii)

13. The chart shows two sets of fractions. Each fraction in group A is paired with an equivalent fraction in group B.

Group A	Group B
28/36	7/9
12/20	3/5
16/28	4/7

Which of these describes the method that can be used to change each fraction in group B to its partner in group A?

(a) Subtract 12 from both the numerator and the denominator

(b) Subtract 26 from both the numerator and the denominator

(c) Multiply both the numerator and the denominator by 4

(d) Divide both the numerator and denominator by $\dfrac{2}{4}$

14. The local pizza place cuts their pizzas into sixths, so that each slice is $\dfrac{1}{6}$ of the pizza. If 8 people share the four pizzas, then the number of slices does each person get will be

(a) 4 (b) 6 (c) 8 (d) 3

15. It takes Jinny $\dfrac{5}{6}$ hour to walk to the playground and $\dfrac{1}{4}$ hour to walk from the playground to school. How much time does it takes Jinny to walk to the playground and then to school?

(a) $\dfrac{12}{19}$ hour (b) $1\dfrac{1}{13}$ hours (c) $1\dfrac{1}{12}$ hours (d) $\dfrac{12}{13}$ hour

Direction (Q. Nos. 16-17) The score of players in a video game is given below :

Ken	Shim	Rose	Jack	Den
$\dfrac{75}{100}$	$\dfrac{46}{50}$	$\dfrac{54}{60}$	$\dfrac{72}{100}$	$\dfrac{89}{100}$

16. Who scored the highest?
(a) Ken (b) Rose
(c) Shim (d) Den

17. What is difference between the score of the winner and the loser?

(a) $\dfrac{1}{5}$ (b) $\dfrac{14}{20}$ (c) $\dfrac{13}{100}$ (d) $\dfrac{15}{40}$

18. Christen uses a cup and a jar to mix juice. It takes 3 cups of juice to fill in the jar. He pours pineapple juice into the jar until it is half full. Then, he adds half a cup of orange juice. How full is the jar now?

(a) One-quater full   (b) Two-third full

(c) Three-fourth full   (d) None of these

19. Victor can kick a football $7\frac{5}{7}$ ft high, Leon can kick the same ball $10\frac{4}{5}$ ft high. How many times far can Victor throw the ball as compared to Leon?

(a) $\frac{2}{3}$ (b) $\frac{7}{4}$ (c) $\frac{5}{7}$ (d) $\frac{2}{5}$

20. Fill in the blanks and choose the correct option.

(i) proper	(ii) like	(iii) $\frac{5}{4}$
(iv) 1	(v) 0	(vi) improper
(vii) unlike		(viii) $\frac{-4}{5}$

I. $\frac{16}{13}$ is a/an .... fraction.

II. The multiplicative inverse of $\frac{4}{5}$ is ....

III. The fractions having different denominators are called .... fractions.

IV. The product of a fractional number and its multiplicative inverse is equal to ....

Codes

	I	II	III	IV		I	II	III	IV
(a)	(vi)	(viii)	(ii)	(iv)	(b)	(i)	(viii)	(vii)	(v)
(c)	(i)	(iii)	(ii)	(v)	(d)	(vi)	(iii)	(vii)	(iv)

21. If Fig. I represents

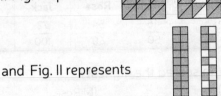

and Fig. II represents .

Then, which of the following is true for the fraction of shaded parts in figures I and II?

(a) I > II   (b) II > I

(c) I = II   (d) I ≤ II

22. Once a young prince asked his gatekeeper to get him an elephant's ride around his father's kingdom. The gatekeeper denied him as he was too young to sit on an elephant. The prince tempted him by saying that he would give $\frac{2}{5}$th of all the coins he had in his pocket. Hearing it, the gatekeeper agreed. If the prince had 35 coins in his pocket, how many coins did he left with after giving it to the gatekeeper?

(a) 14   (b) 21   (c) 28   (d) 35

23. State 'T' for true and 'F' for false and mark the correct option.

I. $\frac{2}{5}$ is equivalent to $2 \times \frac{1}{5}$.

II. Fifteen $\frac{1}{10}$'s make $2\frac{2}{5}$.

III. represent $3\frac{1}{2}$, if $\blacksquare$ = 1.

IV. $\frac{2}{3}, \frac{4}{6}, \frac{18}{27}$ are all improper fractions.

	I	II	III	IV		I	II	III	IV
(a)	F	F	T	T	(b)	F	T	F	T
(c)	T	F	T	F	(d)	T	T	F	F

24. Nomani works 15 hours a week (Monday to Friday). Last week she worked $3\frac{1}{2}$ hours on Monday, 4 hours on Tuesday, $2\frac{1}{6}$ hours on Wednesday and $1\frac{1}{2}$ on Thursday.

How many hours did she work on Friday?

(a) 4 hours   (b) $\frac{5}{6}$ hour   (c) $3\frac{5}{6}$ hours (d) $2\frac{5}{6}$ hours

25. Jessica and Denmark each shaded some parts of two squares of the same size as given below.

Jessica's square   Denmark's square

Andrew, their friend, also shaded some parts of a square of the same size where he shaded a greater area than Jessica but a smaller area than Denmark. Which of the following can be Andrew's square?

(a) (b) (c) (d)

CHAPTER 5

Decimals

Decimal numbers   The numbers in which decimal point is used are called decimal numbers.

Decimal place value chart

Thousand	Hundred	Tens	Ones	Decimal point	Tenth	Hundredth	Thousandth
1000	100	10	1	•	$\dfrac{1}{10}$	$\dfrac{1}{100}$	$\dfrac{1}{1000}$

Expanded form of decimals   It represents the decimal numbers in the form of addition of place values of the digits with respect to their position.

e.g.   Expanded form of 471.231 is $4 \times 100 + 7 \times 10 + 1 \times 1 + \dfrac{2}{10} + \dfrac{3}{100} + \dfrac{1}{1000}$

Converting Decimals into Fractions

✦ Count the number of digits to the right of the decimal point.

✦ Write the decimal number without decimal point as numerator of the fraction and in the denominator write '1' in place of decimal point and as many zeroes to the right of 1 as the number of digits to the right of decimal point.

e.g.   Converting 246.231 into fraction, we get

$$246.231 = \dfrac{246231}{1000}$$

Comparison of Decimal Numbers

✦ Compare the integral part (whole number part) first, ignoring the decimal point.

✦ If the integral part is same, then first convert the decimal numbers in like decimals and then compare the decimal part.

Let's Practice

1. Harry distributed 236 kg of wheat into 16 people equally, then the quantity of wheat each people will get
(a) 25.63 kg (b) 16.75 kg
(c) 17.85 kg (d) 14.75 kg

2. If $A = 31.36$ and $B = 45.63$. Then, the value of $(2A - B)$ is equal to
(a) 17.09 (b) 30.70 (c) 18.79 (d) 23.63

3. The Queen Mary school had its sports day. The five children who participated in long jump have the following record of jumps :

Alex	4.50 m
Amena	4.06 m
Ornald	3.99 m
Florence	3.09 m
Giba	4.28 m

Who won the long jump competition?
(a) Alex (b) Ornald (c) Giba (d) Florence

4. The shaded parts of this picture show what decimal number?

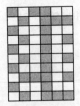

Each ☐ = 0.02

(a) 0.42 (b) 0.58 (c) 0.28 (d) 0.29

5. What number is modelled in the place value chart given below?

Thousand	Hundred	Tens	Ones	Tenth	Hundredth	Thousandth

(a) 3529.035 (b) 3529.35
(c) 3511.035 (d) 3511.35

6. A bill collection machine round off the numbers correct to two decimal places and then give the result. What will be the output of that machine?

Input	Output
4.123	–
7.299	–
14.756	–
0.014	–

(a) 4.12, 7.30, 14.76, 0.01 (b) 4.13, 7.29, 14.76, 0.02
(c) 4.3, 7.20, 14.8, 0.1 (d) None of these

7. Six friends collected sugar for the cake competition to be held next day. Arrange these bags according to their weight from the lightest to the heaviest and choose the correct option.

£6.18 £6.08 £6.81 £6.10 £6.80

(a) 6.18 < 6.08 < 6.81 < 6.10 < 6.80
(b) 6.08 < 6.10 < 6.18 < 6.80 < 6.81
(c) 6.10 < 6.18 < 6.08 < 6.80 < 6.81
(d) None of the above

8. Miss. Julia went for shopping to buy a pair of jeans, a black shirt and a brown bag. The cost of these things at different shops are given below :

	Jeans	Shirt	Bag
Shop 1	₹ 1147.21	₹ 534.23	₹ 520.12
Shop 2	₹ 1272.46	₹ 324.49	₹ 420.41
Shop 3	₹ 1014.76	₹ 576.23	₹ 500.29

From which shop shall she buy the things to have a minimum bill of the items, considering that she buys all the items from one shop only?
(a) Shop 1 (b) Shop 2
(c) Shop 3 (d) Cannot be determined

9. Andrew asked her sister to measure his height. Her sister after measuring Andrew's height said, "You have to grow 35 cm more to reach 2.5 m height."

On the basis of his sister's comment, what is the present height of Andrew?

(a) 0.6 m   (b) 1.25 m   (c) 2.15 m   (d) 2.85 m

10. Marshall asked his friends, "how can you tell if a number is greater than another number on a number line?" His friends said the following statements.

Minti The number to the right is always a greater number.

Krish The number to the left is always a greater number.

Cathy The number to the right is always a two-digit number.

Den There is no way to know.

Who said the correct statement?

(a) Minti   (b) Krish   (c) Cathy   (d) Den

11. What is the sum of the numbers represented by the letters A and B marked on the number line given below?

(a) 14.05   (b) 16.71   (c) 14.15   (d) 16.19

12. In the following magical stairs, a relation given between the numbers on stair, find the missing number and choose the correct option.

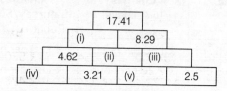

	(i)	(ii)	(iii)	(iv)	(v)
(a)	8.79	6.5	2.79	2.41	3.19
(b)	9.21	5.5	3.29	0.41	2.29
(c)	9.12	4.5	3.79	1.41	1.29
(d)	None of the above				

13. State 'T' for true and 'F' for false and choose the correct option.

I. 15.73 rounded to nearest tenth is equal to 15.7.

II. 6 hundredth is written as 0.60.

III. The digit 5 in 24.56 stands for 5 hundredths.

IV. 0.023 lies between 0.2 and 0.3.

	I	II	III	IV		I	II	III	IV
(a)	T	F	F	F	(b)	F	T	T	F
(c)	T	F	F	T	(d)	F	T	T	T

Direction (Q. Nos. 14-15) Four identical paint pots of 2 L are being used by the painter and the following quantity of paint is left behind.

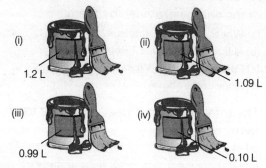

14. What is the total quantity of paint left?

(a) 3.38 L   (b) 3.9 L   (c) 4.2 L   (d) 13.99 L

15. The difference between the maximum and minimum quantity of paint used is

(a) 0.99 L   (b) 1.1 L   (c) 1.09 L   (d) 1.2 L

16. Fill in the blanks and choose the correct option.

(i) 0.90	(ii) 0.24
(iii) 9.01	(iv) 9.1
(v) 9.07	(vi) 9.0
(vii) 0.06	(viii) 0.625

I. The fraction $\dfrac{6}{25}$ is equal to decimal number _____.

II. 15.8 – 6.73 is equal to _____.

III. 9.07 rounded off to nearest tenth is _____.

IV. 9.037 rounded off to nearest tenth is _____.

	I	II	III	IV
(a)	(viii)	(v)	(vii)	(iv)
(b)	(viii)	(iii)	(v)	(i)
(c)	(ii)	(vi)	(iii)	(iv)
(d)	(ii)	(v)	(iv)	(vi)

Direction (Q. Nos. 17-18) Energy contents of different foods are as follow :

Food	Energy content per kg
Wheat	4.25 J
Rice	4.31 J
Potatoes (Cooked)	4.72 J
Milk	4.09 J

17. Arrange the food items in ascending order of the energy provided by them.
    (a) Wheat < Rice < Potatoes < Milk
    (b) Milk < Wheat < Rice < Potatoes
    (c) Potatoes < Rice < Wheat < Milk
    (d) None of the above

18. The total energy provided by all the food items is
    (a) 14.37 J
    (b) 15.74 J
    (c) 17.37 J
    (d) None of these

Direction (Q. Nos. 19-20) The table given below shows the mass of children when they were born.

Children	Mass (in kg)
Emma	4.65
Joy	3.75
Zua	5.25
Tim	3.59
Luca	4.96

19. What is the difference in mass of Emma and Zua?
    (a) 0.50 kg   (b) 600 g   (c) 750 g   (d) 1 kg

20. The total mass of Joy and Luca together is
    (a) 9.01 kg   (b) 8 kg   (c) 8.50 kg   (d) 8.71 kg

21. ITSC Bank provide the following list of value of other currency in Indian rupees :

Country	Currency	Value (in ₹)
Sri Lanka	Rupee (SL)	0.37
USA	Dollar	60.23
UAE	Dirham	11.40
England	Pound	93.75
Hong Kong	Dollar (HK)	6.20
China	Yuan	6.75

Brian living in England gets a pocket money of 15 pounds. He transferred ₹ 375.50 to his Indian friend to buy an Indian painting for himself. How much money (in Indian rupees) is left with Brian now?
(a) ₹ 900.25 (b) ₹ 1681.25 (c) ₹ 1771.75 (d) ₹ 1030.75

Direction (Q. Nos. 22-23) Tyran and his two younger sisters, of age 9 years and 10 years respectively, are going to see a movie that starts at quarter to 6.

Cinema 1	Cinema 2
Invasion from Mars 12:30, 2:15, 4:00, 5:45, 7:30, 9:15	The Museum Mystery 12:45, 2:30, 4:15, 6:00, 7:45, 9:30
Adults ₹ 6.00 Children (under 12) ₹ 3.75	

22. Tyran is paying for the three tickets. He is 9 years older than his youngest sister. How much will he spend for tickets?
    (a) ₹ 18.25   (b) ₹ 16.75   (c) ₹ 13.5   (d) ₹ 13.75

23. Tyran and his sisters plan on spending a total of ₹ 2.75 for snacks whereas their parents plan on spending a total of ₹ 4.35. What will be the total cost of tickets and snacks for the entire family?
    (a) ₹ 32.6
    (b) ₹ 28.1
    (c) ₹ 30.75
    (d) None of these

Direction (Q. Nos. 24-25) Divine parked his bike from 10 am to 6 : 50 pm on Monday and Sunday. The charges of parking are given below :

Time	Charges (weekdays)	Charges (Saturday/Sunday Public holidays)
6 am to 11 am	₹ 1.50 per hour	₹ 1.20 per hour
11 am to 5 pm	₹ 2.20 per hour	₹ 1.80 per hour
5 pm onwards	₹ 0.50 every $\frac{1}{2}$ hour or part thereof	₹ 2.20 per half hour

24. How much did Divine have to pay in total for the parking charges on Monday?
    (a) ₹ 16.7   (b) ₹ 10.5   (c) ₹ 28.4   (d) ₹ 4.2

25. How much cheaper did he pay for the parking charges on Sunday than on Monday?
    (a) ₹ 0.1
    (b) ₹ 4.1
    (c) ₹ 4.2
    (d) None of these

Geometry

Angle   A shape, formed by two lines or rays diverging from a common point.

Types of Angle

+ **Acute angle**   An angle with measure between 0° and 90° is called an acute angle.
+ **Right angle**   An angle with measure equal to 90° is called a right angle.
+ **Obtuse angle**   An angle with measure between 90° and 180° is called an obtuse angle.
+ **Straight angle**   An angle with measure equal to 180° is called a straight angle.

Open shape   An open shape is made up of line segments but there is atleast one line segment that is not connected to any line segment at one of its end points.

Closed shape   A closed figure is a figure that begins and ends at the same point.

Polygon   A plane figure with atleast three sides and angles.

Polygons with different number of sides

Number of sides	Polygon
3	Triangle
4	Quadrilateral
5	Pentagon
6	Hexagon
7	Septagon

Note   Sum of the measure of all three angles of a triangle is 180°.

Let's Practice

1. Richard uses matchsticks and forms some shapes with them. Which of the shapes formed by him is different from others?

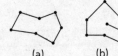 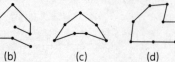

(a)   (b)   (c)   (d)

2. A hunter throws an arrow to kill a deer but it lands on the ground as shown in the picture. What type of angle does it make with the ground?

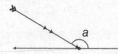

(a) Obtuse   (b) Right

(c) Straight   (d) Acute

3. Pick the odd one out from the following sign boards on the basis of the angle formed.

(a)   (b)   (c)   (d)

4. Choose the correct matched option from the following.

Column A		Column B	
I.	$\triangleleft a$	(i)	Obtuse angle
II.		(ii)	Acute angle
III.		(iii)	Right angle
IV.		(iv)	Obtuse angle

	I	II	III	IV
(a)	(ii)	(iv)	(i)	(iii)
(b)	(i)	(ii)	(iii)	(iv)
(c)	(iv)	(i)	(ii)	(iii)
(d)	(ii)	(iii)	(iv)	(i)

5. A road map of an area is given below. It has 4 roads drawn. Which of the angles marked in the map is an obtuse angle?

(a) Angle *a*   (b) Angle *b*   (c) Angle *c*   (d) Angle *d*

6. Compare the following shapes on the basis of the number of right angles in each one and choose the correct option.

(a) I > II > III (b) I < II < III (c) II > III > I (d) III > II > I

7. The base of a stretcher is made strong by joining the rods making angles of different measure. Choose which of the angle formed in the figure is an obtuse angle?

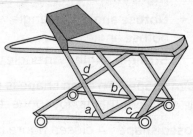

(a) Angle *b*   (b) Angle *c*   (c) Angle *d*   (d) Angle *a*

8. Shane drew some shapes and asked his friends to find the difference between them.

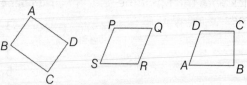

Jenny They are all same.

Kim They have equal sides and equal angles.

Kandy They have equal number of sides but different angles.

Who said the correct statement?

(a) Jenny

(b) Kim

(c) Kandy

(d) None of these

9.

Mr. Nene wrote a name on the blackboard and asked the students to count the number of acute angles formed. Four students stood up and had different answers as follows

Neil   There are nine acute angles.

Shimer   There are twelve acute angles.

Jany   There are ten acute angles.

Trini   There are fifteen acute angles.

Who is correct in counting the number of acute angles?

(a) Neil

(b) Shimer

(c) Jany

(d) Trini

10. In an activity class, the students were asked to half fold the paper three times and then unfold it as shown below :

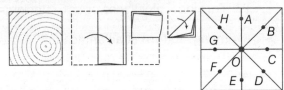

Now, the students were asked to count the number of right angles formed. What would be the correct number of right angles formed in the above activity?

(a) 4

(b) 6

(c) 8

(d) 10

11. The picture given below shows the different angles made by the line joining the tip of a stick with the tip of the shadow at different times of a day.

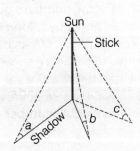

Which of the following statements is true about the angles *a*, *b* and *c*?

   I. All are right angles .

   II. Only *a* and *c* are acute angles.

   III. All are acute angles.

   IV. Only *a* and *c* are obtuse angles.

(a) II

(b) I

(c) IV

(d) III

12. Points, *P, Q, R, S* and *T* lie on a polygon as shown below :

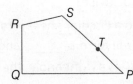

Which of the following tables classifies the angles of the polygon correctly?

(a)

Angle	Type
P	Obtuse
Q	Straight
R	Acute
S	Acute
T	Right

(b)

Angle	Type
P	Acute
Q	Right
R	Obtuse
S	Obtuse
T	Straight

(c)

Angle	Type
P	Acute
Q	Straight
R	Obtuse
S	Right
T	Right

(d)

Angle	Type
P	Acute
Q	Straight
R	Obtuse
S	Obtuse
T	Right

13. The hour hand of the clock given below is turned 90° clockwise and then 180° anti-clockwise. Which angle will be formed by the minutes and hour hands of the clock after rotation?

(a) 45°

(b) 90°

(c) 180°

(d) None of these

14. Fill in the blanks and choose the correct option.

(i) 90°	(ii) 180°
(iii) 270°	(iv) 45°
(v) 42°	(vi) 41°

  I. Half of a right angle is _____ .

  II. Turning $\frac{3}{4}$ anti-clockwise means turning by an angle of measure _____ anti-clockwise.

  III. Folding a circular sheet into halves two times will form a _____ angle.

  IV. If ∠ABC is a right angle, then ∠DBE is equal to _____ .

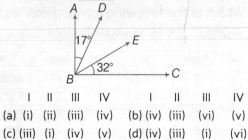

	I	II	III	IV		I	II	III	IV
(a)	(i)	(ii)	(iii)	(iv)	(b)	(iv)	(iii)	(vi)	(v)
(c)	(iii)	(i)	(iv)	(v)	(d)	(iv)	(iii)	(i)	(vi)

15. Sindri, the spider is having trouble in making his webs. He likes his web angles to be a perfect 90° angle. Find the missing angles to complete his web and choose the correct option.

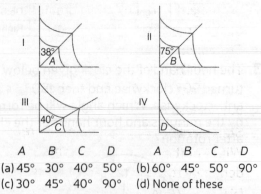

	A	B	C	D		A	B	C	D
(a)	45°	30°	40°	50°	(b)	60°	45°	50°	90°
(c)	30°	45°	40°	90°	(d)	None of these			

16. Triangles are rigid strong structures used for rafters in buildings and curved domes. Engineers use this shape in making bridges. One of them is given in the picture below

The bridge is made up of same type of angles as shown below

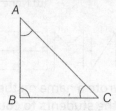

If one angle is right angle and the other two angles are equal, then the sum of the measure of the other two angles is
(a) 30°   (b) 45°
(c) 60°   (d) 90°

17. State 'T' for true and 'F' for false and choose the correct option.

  I. Different shapes can be formed using same number of sides.

  II. Alphabet 'L' forms a right angle.

  III. A rectangle and a square have equal angles.

  IV. Turning $\frac{1}{4}$ clockwise or anti-clockwise means to turn at an angle 90°.

	I	II	III	IV		I	II	III	IV
(a)	T	T	F	F	(b)	F	F	T	T
(c)	F	F	F	F	(d)	T	T	T	T

18.

Martin's protractor got ruined and the impression of some numbers got faded. He had to draw an angle by taking OB as base but mistakenly he took OA as base and drew an angle of measure shown in the figure. If he had to draw the same angle with OB as base, then what would be the measure of it with OA as base?
(a) 120°   (b) 130°
(c) 70°   (d) 50°

19. Max went to the playground to get rides. He liked playground slides the more, so he went on sliding on two different slides having different slopes, based on the angle made with the ground.

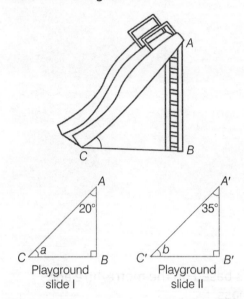

Playground slide I   Playground slide II

The angles made by each slide with the ground are
(a) 70°, 45°   (b) 80°, 65°
(c) 70°, 55°   (d) 80°, 45°

20.

I.   II.

III.   IV.

The clocks given in figures show different time. On the basis of it, different angles are formed between the hour hand and the minute hand.

Find the angle formed between the hands and choose the correct option.
(a) 90°, 75°, 130°, 115°
(b) 90°, 65°, 125°, 110°
(c) 100°, 50°, 135°, 80°
(d) None of the above

Direction (Q. Nos. 21-22)

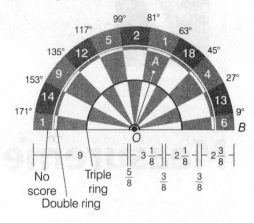

A dart board is 18 inch across. It is divided into twenty wedges of equal size. The score of a mark is indicated by numbers around the board. Only the top of the dart board is shown.

21. Michael gets two turns to get a score of 18 such that the sum of his score should not exceed 18 in order to win. If in the first chance he scores 4, then at which angle he should land his dart to win the game?

Statement I At any angle greater than 152° but not more than 170°.

Statement II At any angle less than or equal to 170°.

Statement III At any angle less than 135° but not less than 116°.

Statement IV At an angle not more than 90°.
Which of the above statements will be definitely true to obtain the score?
(a) I   (b) II   (c) III   (d) IV

22. If Sandy's first and second aim always land between the angles 46° to 90° and 100° to 130° respectively, then what would be the maximum score she can get?
(a) 25   (b) 30   (c) 23   (d) 20

CHAPTER
7

Measurement

Metric system The decimal measuring system is based on the metre, litre and gram as units of length, capacity and weight or mass.

+ The basic unit of length is metre (m).
+ The basic unit of weight is gram (g).
+ The basic unit of capacity is litre (L).

The basic conversion formulae for the units of length, weight and capacity are

+ 100 cm = 1 m   + 1000 m = 1 km   + 1000 mg = 1 g
+ 1000 g = 1 kg   + 1000 mL = 1 L   + 1000 L = 1 kL

Cube It is a solid figure with 6 square surfaces.

Cuboid It is a solid figure with 6 rectangular surfaces.

Volume It is the space occupied by an object. It is measured in cubic units.

e.g.   Volume of cuboid = Length × Breadth × Height

Volume of cube = Edge × Edge × Edge

Temperature It is a measure of the warmness or coldness of an object.

The units of temperature are celsius and fahrenheit.

Conversion formulae for temperature

$$°C = (°F - 32) × \frac{5}{9}, \quad °F = \left(°C × \frac{9}{5}\right) + 32$$

Let's Practice

1. Ella walked once around the given track. How far did Ella walk?

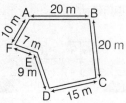

(a) 810 cm   (b) 8100 cm

(c) 81 cm   (d) None of these

2. If $°C = (°F - 32) \times \dfrac{5}{9}$, then what is the temperature shown by the given thermometer in celsius?

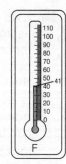

(a) 10°C

(b) 5°C

(c) 23°C

(d) 18°C

3. In Banaras and Kolkata, women wear sarees of length 8.28 m long. If a yard is equal to 0.92 m. Then, how much do they measure their sarees in yards?

(a) 8 yards   (b) 7 yards   (c) 9 yards   (d) 6 yards

4. Study the following diagram. If the weight of 1 square = 5 circles and 1 triangle = 4 circles, then the number of circles required on the other side of the scale to balance the scale is

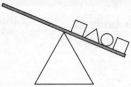

(a) 12   (b) 15   (c) 21   (d) 3

5. Braiden have to bake a cake for his sister's birthday party. He noted down the recipe from internet and started preparing for it. The recipe instructed to bake the batter to 212°F but Braiden have a microwave with temperature given in celsius. What would be the temperature (in celsius) at which he should bake the batter?

(a) 0°C   (b) 70°C   (c) 100°C   (d) 212°C

6. Stephanie stacked toy blocks to form the shape as shown below:

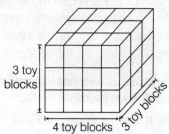

How many toy blocks are in Stephanie's stack of toy blocks?

(a) 12   (b) 24   (c) 36   (d) 48

7. Angelina planted rose flowers on the boundary of her house. She has placed the plants 8 cm apart from each other.

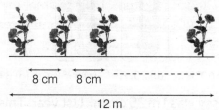

If the length of the boundary and the sequence of plants is as given above, then how many such plants can be planted?

(a) 150   (b) 151   (c) 160   (d) 164

8. Maxin wanted to find the volume of a spherical ball but could not remember the formula. He then used a measuring glass and pour some water in it.

After dropping the ball in the glass, the water is raised to level as shown below

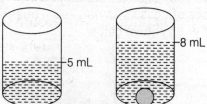

If $1\,mL = 1\,cm^3$, then what is the volume (in cm^3) of ball?

(a) 5   (b) 3

(c) 8   (d) 13

9. Michelle bought a shirt for her brother but some how its length was short. Her brother asked her to get it exchanged and buy a shirt of length 4 inch greater than this. If the length of the shirt is 58.5 cm, then what is the length of the shirt Michelle's brother want? (given, 1 inch = 2.5 cm)

(a) 95.5 cm   (b) 48.9 cm
(c) 68.5 cm   (d) 58.9 cm

10. Temperature of two hot vessels containing water is shown below

What is the difference (in °F) of the temperature of the vessels?

$$\left[if\ °F = °C \times \frac{9}{5} + 32 \right]$$

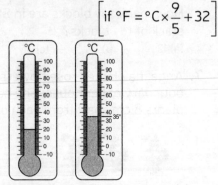

(a) 60°F   (b) 20°F   (c) 59°F   (d) 39°F

11. Jessy was 1 m 25 cm tall last year. This year, he is 12 cm taller. How much taller is Jessy than Teresa now, if Teresa is 1 m 8 cm tall?

(a) 10 cm   (b) 25 cm   (c) 29 cm   (d) 10 cm

12. Aleena had two pieces of gold as 6 kg 755 g and 5 kg 550 g, respectively. She wanted to get a gold biscuit weighing 15 kg. How much more gold does she need?

(a) 1 kg 795 g   (b) 2 kg 795 g
(c) 1 kg 695 g   (d) 2 kg 675 g

13. Two cubical boxes are dipped into two same types of vessels having equal quantity of water as shown below

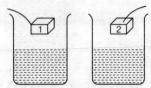

If the dimensions of box 1 is 2 cm × 3 cm × 4 cm and of box 2 is 3.5 cm × 1.5 cm × 0.05 m, then in which of the given vessels will the water raise to more height?

(a) Both the box will have same height of raised water
(b) Box 2
(c) Box 1
(d) Cannot be determined

14. If object $\boxed{C}$ weighs 4 kg 800 g, then find the mass of object $\boxed{B}$.

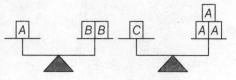

(a) 500 g   (b) 600 g
(c) 800 g   (d) 1000 g

15. Every teacher is assigned with a school locker to keep their books and notebooks. If the volume of one book is 24 cubic inch, then the number of such books can be placed in the locker is

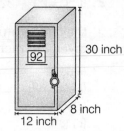

(a) 100   (b) 120
(c) 150   (d) 160

16. Fill in the blanks and choose the correct option.

(i) 100	(ii) 32	(iii) 212	(iv) 95
(v) 35	(vi) 50	(vii) 10	

I. Water freezes at 0°C which is same as _____ °F.

II. Water boils at _____ °F which is same as 100°C.

III. 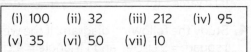 _____ °F temperature is shown by the thermometer.

IV. The difference of 35°C and 25°C in fahrenheit is _____ .

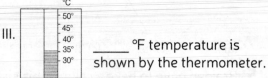

(a) (ii) (iii) (iv) (vi)
(b) (iii) (i) (v) (vi)
(c) (iii) (ii) (vi) (v)
(d) None of the above

17. How many △ do you need to balance the set up given below?

If 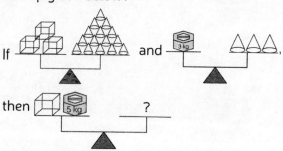 and ,

then 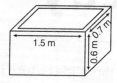 ?

(a) 9△ (b) 10△ (c) 12△ (d) 15△

18. If ten buckets of same volume are used to fill the given bath tub, then the volume of one such bucket is

(given, $1 m^3 = 1000$ L)

1.5 m | 0.6 m | 0.7 m

(a) 63 L (b) 6.3 L
(c) 630 L (d) None of these

19. A big cube shaped brick of gold is melted to make small cuboid shaped biscuits of measure 30 cm × 20 cm × 0.05 m. If the edge of the brick measures 1.2 m, then the number of such biscuits can be formed is

(a) 600 (b) 696
(c) 472 (d) None of these

20. State 'T' for true and 'F' for false and choose the correct option.

I. Mixing 3.6 kg of orange candy with 0.75 kg of yellow candy and packing them in 5 boxes of equal weight will make each box of weight 0.87 kg.

II. If Vandy having height $1\frac{3}{8}$ m is $\frac{1}{4}$ m shorter than Andy, then Andy is $1\frac{1}{8}$ m tall.

III. If 13338 L of oil is poured in 9 cans equally, then weight of each can is 14.82 L.

IV. Length of a book is measured in litres.

	I	II	III	IV		I	II	III	IV
(a)	F	T	F	F	(b)	T	F	F	F
(c)	F	F	F	F	(d)	T	T	F	T

21. Martini have a big bucket. He needs to put 1 L of water in it for his science enquiry but he only have 150 mL and 25 mL containers. How many times does he need to use each of the container to fill in the bucket?

(a) 150 mL → 4 times   25 mL → 6 times
(b) 150 mL → 8 times   25 mL → 3 times
(c) 150 mL → 6 times   25 mL → 4 times
(d) None of the above

Direction (Q. Nos. 22-23) George, Greg and Han decided to make ice-cream for their friend's birthday party. Copying down the instructions from internet, they went to market to buy the following products.

Whipped cream	1 L
Condensed milk	500 mL
Sugar	250 g

22. If the cream costs ₹ 400 and is in 200 mL pots. How much money did they spend on buying the required amount of cream?

(a) ₹ 1000 (b) ₹ 2000 (c) ₹ 1500 (d) ₹ 2400

23. The condensed milk costs ₹ 250.50 for every 200 mL. If they only got $\frac{3}{5}$ of the milk required for the recipe, then how much money did they spend?

(a) ₹ 275.75 (b) ₹ 375.75
(c) ₹ 305.50 (d) None of these

24. Mr. Gredwick and his workers had to pack 140 cubical shape boxes to be delivered to a shop. They made three boxes having square box of sides 30 ft, 20 ft and 10 ft respectively and having equal height of 12 ft each. If all the boxes got completely packed without leaving any space, then what would be the volume (in cubic ft) of each of the small box?

(a) 120 (b) 140 (c) 160 (d) 180

25. For every 220 mL of lemon juice, a drink seller mixes it with 770 mL of water to make lemonade. The drink seller has 2 bottles of lemon juice. Each bottle contains 1100 mL of lemon juice. How much lemonade can he make?

(a) 9 L 900 mL (b) 9009 mL
(c) 9.9 mL (d) None of these

Pattern and Symmetry

Symmetry means when one shape does not change, if you flip, slide or turn it.

Line of symmetry   It is the line which divides a figure into two congruent parts, each of which are same in shape and size.

e.g.

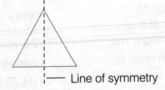

—— Line of symmetry

Mirror image   It is the image of an object which is identical to it but with the structure reversed, as in a mirror.

Mirror

Rotational symmetry   A shape has rotational symmetry, when it still looks same after a rotation ($\frac{1}{2}$ turn, $\frac{1}{4}$ turn, less than one full turn).

Some Important Facts

✦ Anti-clockwise turn → Turning toward left side
✦ Clockwise turn → Turning toward right side
✦ $\frac{1}{2}$ turn → Turning at 180° angle   ✦ $\frac{1}{4}$ turn → Turning at 90° angle
✦ $\frac{1}{3}$ turn → Turning at 120° angle   ✦ $\frac{1}{6}$ turn → Turning at 60° angle

Pattern   It refers to a rule followed by a series of numbers or letters or image.

Let's Practice

1. Brindy was playing with a toy ball by rotating it in a pattern as shown below

If she rotates it again, how would the ball look like?

(a)   (b)

(c)   (d) None of these

2. In an art class, a teacher taught students how to make symmetrical pattern by blotting ink and then folding the paper. One of the student tried the activity and formed a shape, half of which is given alongside.

The correct pattern of the other half of the paper will be

(a)   (b)

(c) Both (a) and (b)   (d) None of these

3. How many axis/lines of symmetry does the given figure have?
(a) 1   (b) 3
(c) 4   (d) 5

4. How many of the following letters have a vertical line of symmetry

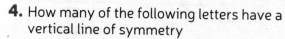

(a) 4   (b) 5
(c) 8   (d) All of these

5. Which of the given below figures will look same on turning a half turn?

(a)   (b)   (c)   (d)

6. If a cross (✘) and a tick (✔) is marked on the figures that are symmetrical and non-symmetrical respectively, then choose the correct option on the basis of it.

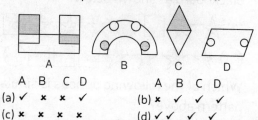

	A	B	C	D

A B C D   A B C D
(a) ✔ ✘ ✘ ✔   (b) ✘ ✔ ✔ ✔
(c) ✘ ✘ ✘ ✘   (d) ✔ ✔ ✔ ✔

7. Mr. Gredwick drew four pictures and asked the students to comment on their properties.

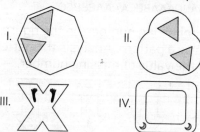

Grish They all are symmetrical.
Kandish Figures I and II have horizontal line of symmetry.
Mindi Fig. III has no line of symmetry.
Tango Fig. IV has vertical line of symmetry.

Who said the correct statement?
(a) Grish and Mindi
(b) Kandish and Tango
(c) Mindi and Tango
(d) None of the above

8. State 'T' for true and 'F' for false and choose the correct option.

I. Every figure has both a vertical and a horizontal line of symmetry.
II. All letters of alphabet series are symmetrical.
III. In the word 'SON' only letter 'O' is not symmetrical.

IV.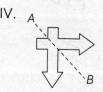

AB is the line of symmetry of the given figure.

	I	II	III	IV		I	II	III	IV
(a)	T	T	F	F	(b)	F	F	F	T
(c)	T	T	T	F	(d)	F	F	T	T

9. Ms. Bernard drew a series of pictures on the blackboard as shown below

Which of the following options is similar to pattern above?

(a) ABC ABC AABC AAB

(b) AABC AABC AAABBC

(c) AA BC AAABC AAAABC

(d) AABCAAABBCAAAABBBCC

10. The following numbers in the figure '▽' follows a pattern. Analysis the pattern and find the value of missing number.

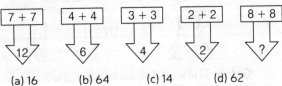

(a) 16   (b) 64   (c) 14   (d) 62

11. What would be the correct next shape for the given pattern?

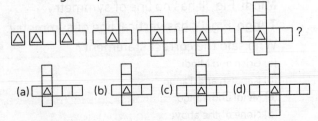

12. The cube shown below was cut into three pieces.

Which of the following groups can be joined to make the given cube.

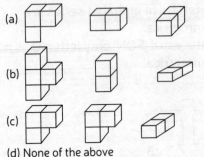

(d) None of the above

13. While arranging her books, Suzane put 3 books on first rack, 6 books on second rack, 12 books on third rack and so on. If she kept the books in the same pattern, then how many books will be kept on fifth rack?

(a) 22

(b) 24

(c) 46

(d) 48

14. If $1 = 0 \times 9 + 1$

$11 = 1 \times 9 + 2$

$1111 = 123 \times 9 + 4$

$1111111 = \underline{\hspace{1cm}} \times 9 + \underline{\hspace{1cm}}$

Then, the missing numbers are

(a) 1234, 5

(b) 12345, 6

(c) 123456, 7

(d) 1234567, 8

15. Match the following columns of solid shapes with their correct net and choose the correct option.

Column A	Column B
I.	(i)
II.	(ii)
III.	(iii)
IV.	(iv)

	I	II	III	IV
(a)	(i)	(ii)	(iv)	(iii)
(b)	(ii)	(i)	(iii)	(iv)
(c)	(iv)	(iii)	(i)	(ii)
(d)	None of the above

16. What is the least number of squares that must be shaded to make the given figure symmetrical about the line *AB*?

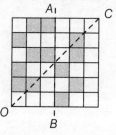

(a) 8   (b) 9   (c) 10   (d) 12

17. If $1+2+3+4+5+6+7+8+9 = 55-10$

and $41+42+43+44+45+46+47$
$+48+49 = 455-50,$

then without actually adding,
$91+92+93+94+95+96+97+98+99$
= _____

(a) $999-90$ (b) $995+10$
(c) $955-100$ (d) Cannot be determined

18. In a vending machine a number of toffees come out when coins of denomination of ₹ 5 are put in, as shown below

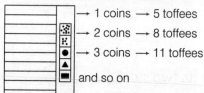

→ 1 coins → 5 toffees
→ 2 coins → 8 toffees
→ 3 coins → 11 toffees
and so on

How many toffees will Sherry get, if she puts in 7 coins each of denomination of ₹ 5?

(a) 17   (b) 23   (c) 39   (d) 53

19.

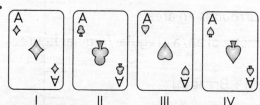

I   II   III   IV

Siddhant while playing with cards placed the above cards on each other while picking up the cards, he turned the pack with half turn and opened each of them one by one. If first the cards were placed as shown above.

Which of the above card will look the same after turning half a turn?

(a) II   (b) III   (c) I   (d) IV

20. Micheal got a homework to draw a pattern of objects.

He drew the following pattern.

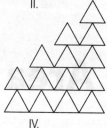

I.   II.   III.   IV.

How many total triangles will be used in the last and second last column of the 17th pattern?

(a) 35   (b) 34   (c) 16   (d) 17

21. While sorting some stationary material Kenya put 58 items in the first box, 69 in the second box, 80 in the third box, 91 in the fourth box and 102 in the fifth box. If this pattern continues, how many items will be their in the 10th box?

(a) 113   (b) 135
(c) 146   (d) 157

22. Martin used triangles and squares to draw a series of pictures as shown below

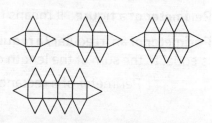

How many triangles will be used in making the 11th picture of this pattern?

(a) 22   (b) 20
(c) 24   (d) Cannot be determined

CHAPTER 9

Area and Perimeter

Area of a figure   It is the total space inside the boundary of a flat two-dimensional object.

Area of a rectangle   Area of a rectangle is the product of its length and breadth.

i.e.   Area = Length × Breadth

Area of a square   Area of a square is the product of its two sides.

i.e.   Area = Side × Side

Perimeter of a figure   It means the path that surrounds an area.

Perimeter of an irregular/a regular figure Perimeter of an/a irregular/regular figure is equal to the sum of the length of its sides.

Perimeter of a rectangle = 2 × (Length + Breadth)

Perimeter of a square = 4 × Side

Let's Practice

1. Mrs. Gerry placed a border around the bulletin board.

The length of the border is an example of
- (a) area
- (b) volume
- (c) perimeter
- (d) circumference

2. Which of the following are the dimensions of a rectangle with a perimeter of 26 inch and an area of 42 sq inch?
- (a) Length-1 inch, width-26 inch
- (b) Length-2 inch, width-13 inch
- (c) Length-2 inch, width-21 inch
- (d) Length-6 inch, width-7 inch

3. Trini has a project to decorate the boundary of a shape given below with a ribbon. How much ribbon will be used to decorate the boundary?

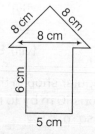

- (a) 40 cm
- (b) 41 cm
- (c) 36 cm
- (d) 32 cm

4. A picture given below shows the area of the land being used for farming in a city. Using this picture, find the area of the land used for farming shown by the shaded portion.

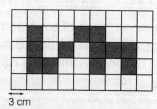

- (a) 108 cm^2
- (b) 72 cm^2
- (c) 12 cm^2
- (d) 9 cm^2

5.

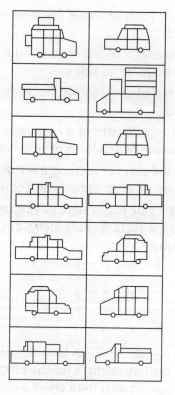

The above parking lot has a fixed space of 2 m × 1 m for each car to be parked. Then, the total area of the parking lot is
- (a) 28 sq m
- (b) 27 sq m
- (c) 11 sq m
- (d) 36 sq m

6. Krish made a windmill for his Science project. He made the blades of the windmill by using wooden sticks of size 6 m. These sticks overlapped each other and formed the square *ABCD*.

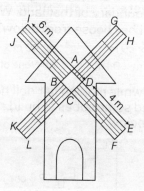

What is the area of the square ABCD, so formed?

(a) 2 m²   (b) 4 m²   (c) 24 m²   (d) 16 m²

7. State 'T' for true and 'F' for false and choose the correct option.

    I. Perimeter of any regular figure is product of its sides.

    II. Area of any regular figure is sum of its sides.

    III. The perimeter of a rectangle formed by joining two squares of side 4 cm is 24 cm.

    IV. If the sides of rectangle are doubled, then its area will also be doubled.

    V. The side of a square having area equal to the rectangle of sides 8 cm by 2 cm is equal to 4 cm.

	I	II	III	IV	V
(a)	F	F	T	F	T
(b)	T	T	T	T	F
(c)	T	F	T	F	F
(d)	F	T	F	T	T

Direction (Q. Nos. 8-9) A king decided to honour his two soldiers for their bravery in the field of war against their enemies. He asked one of them to choose any shape of land having a boundary of measure 100 m.

8. What type of land the soldier must choose in order to have the maximum area of land?

(a) Rectangle   (b) Square

(c) $\frac{1}{2}$ rectangle $+\frac{1}{2}$ square   (d) None of these

9. The king asked the other soldier to choose a land having area equal to 400 m² and he will give him as much length of silver wire as the boundary of that land. Which type of land will he choose from below?

(a) 20 m × 20 m   (b) 40 m × 10 m

(c) 4000 m × 0.1 m   (d) None of these

10. Jessica while making her doll house, arranged some cubes to build stairs for it as shown below

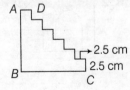

What is the perimeter of the corner ABCD of the stairs, if the dimensions are as given in figure?

(a) 45 cm

(b) 60 cm

(c) 30 cm

(d) Cannot be determined

11. Ecle made a staircase using her toy blocks as given in the picture. If each square block is a cube of edge 1 cm. Then, what is the volume of the total number of cubes/blocks upto the 10th step?

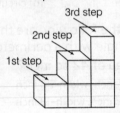

(a) 40 cubic cm   (b) 45 cubic cm

(c) 55 cubic cm   (d) 60 cubic cm

12. Fill in the blanks and choose the correct option.

(i) 1080	(ii) 36
(iii) 160	(iv) 144
(v) 980	(vi) 26
(vii) 72	(viii) 80

    I. A rectangular shop in the mall having dimensions 10 m by 16 m has area _____ sq m.

    II. Area of square having length of one side measures 12 m is equal to _____ sq m.

    III. The length of a rectangle is $\frac{6}{5}$th of its breadth. If its perimeter is 132 m, its area will be _____ sq m.

    IV. The dimensions of a rectangle having length 10 m and breadth 8 m is doubled, then its new perimeter is equal to _____ m.

	I	II	III	IV
(a)	(vi)	(vii)	(v)	(viii)
(b)	(iii)	(iv)	(i)	(vii)
(c)	(viii)	(ii)	(iv)	(vii)
(d)	(iv)	(iii)	(vi)	(ii)

13. Maria had a length of wire 40 cm long. She bent the wire to make the following shape, where X and Y are squares.

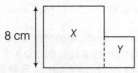

8 cm

What is the area (in cm^2) of square Y?

(a) 6 (b) 9

(c) 16 (d) 24

14. Jolly and Ted built pens for their dogs as given in the picture.

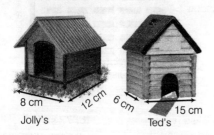

8 cm 12 cm 6 cm 15 cm

Jolly's Ted's

Who among them used more fencing to build the bottom of the pen?

(a) Ted

(b) Jolly

(c) Both will use same

(d) Cannot be determined

15. The given shape is formed by using 10 rectangles and the shape is 8 cm wide.

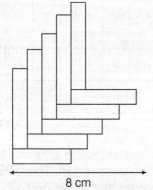

8 cm

What is the perimeter of this shape?

(a) 24 cm

(b) 28 cm

(c) 34 cm

(d) 36 cm

16. A basketball match is to be held next week at South hall united. For this, the floor of the basketball court is to be painted. If 2 L of paint is needed to paint 150 sq ft of the court. Then, how much paint is required to complete the painting of floor?

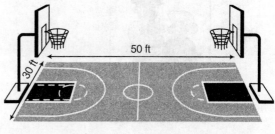

50 ft

30 ft

(a) 10 L (b) 20 L (c) 200 L (d) 150 L

17. Bandy needs to make rectangular invitation cards for her birthday party. She has to cut a square sheet of poster board measuring 12 inch on each side. What is the greatest number of cards that Bandy can make?

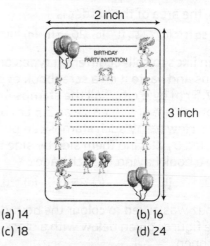

2 inch

BIRTHDAY PARTY INVITATION

3 inch

(a) 14 (b) 16

(c) 18 (d) 24

18. A wire is cut into several smaller pieces. Each of the smaller pieces are bent into two squares. The perimeter of square I and area of square II are as follow :

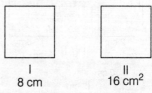

I II
8 cm 16 cm^2

What is the length of the wire?

(a) 20 cm (b) 12 cm

(c) 24 cm (d) 18 cm

19. Mrs. Bishop wanted to make a frame for her family picture. She marked the picture to help her figure out the perimeter of the picture. What is the perimeter of Mrs. Bishop picture?

Scale
⊢—⊣ = 1 cm

(a) 54 cm   (b) 30 cm
(c) 28 cm   (d) 60 cm

20. Addison placed a carpet on the floor of his drawing room but found it to be of the exact size. He wanted to leave a border of 2 ft on each side. If the carpet measures 8 ft by 6 ft. Then, the area of the border is

(a) 48 sq ft   (b) 72 sq ft   (c) 120 sq ft   (d) 100 sq ft

21. Martin likes to collect different types of stamps and paste it on a scrapbook of page size 7.5 cm by 6 cm. If all the stamps in a scrapbook are of same size as 2.5 cm by 1.5 cm. How many such stamps can be collected by placing them side by side in a scrap a book having 10 such pages?

(a) 100   (b) 110   (c) 125   (d) 120

22. Mihinaz was asked to colour the boundary of the figures given below with a black sketchpen.

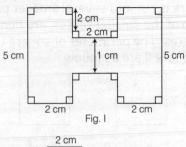

Fig. I

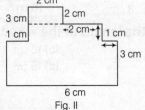

Fig. II

In which figure she needs to colour the boundary more?

(a) I   (b) II
(c) Both I and II   (d) Cannot be determined

23. A classroom of dimensions 18 ft by 22 ft had 28 benches each of size 4 ft and 2.5 ft, an almirah of dimensions 5 ft by 4 ft and a table of size 3 ft by 5 ft. How much space is left in the class room now?

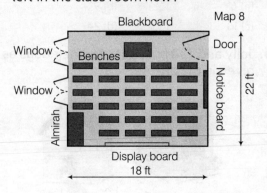

(a) 81 sq ft   (b) 72 sq ft
(c) None of these   (d) Cannot be determined

Direction (Q. Nos. 24-25) A map of school is given in the picture. Answer the following questions on the basis of it considering that each class has same area and dimensions.

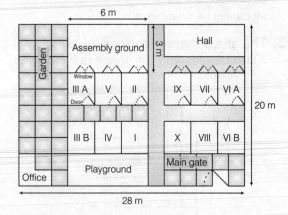

24. If each class has same area and length of each of the class is 4 m. Then, what is the area covered by classes given in the picture?

(a) 12 m²   (b) 8 m²   (c) 96 m²   (d) 144 m²

25. If area of hall is $\frac{2}{3}$ times the area of assembly ground, then what is the perimeter of the hall?

(a) 16 m²   (b) 4 m²   (c) 22 m²   (d) 26 m²

CHAPTER
10

Data Handling

A collection of facts and figures is called data. Data put together as they are collected, are called raw data.

Raw data have to be arranged in some order to make sense. There are many ways of arranging and presenting (showing) data.

Pictograph   It is the visual presentation of data using icons, pictures, symbols, etc.

Bar graph   It is a graph drawn by using rectangular bars to show how large each value is.

Line graph   It is a graph that uses line segments to connect data points.

Pie chart   It is a type of circular chart divided into sectors, where each sector shows the relative size of each value.

Tally marks   It is a mark used in recording a number of acts or objects most often in series of five, consisting of four vertical lines cancelled diagonally by a fifth line.

e.g. $1 = |$ $= |$

$2 = ||$ $= \sqcap$

$3 = |||$ $= \sqcap$

$4 = ||||$ $= \square$

$5 = |||\!|$ $= \boxslash$

Let's Practice

1. A group of friends drew a graph depicting the number of books read by them this year. What is the difference between the maximum and minimum number of books read by friends?

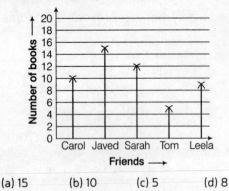

(a) 15   (b) 10   (c) 5   (d) 8

2. If one symbol of 🥛 represents 10 glasses of chocolate milk, then 45 glasses of chocolate milk are represented by

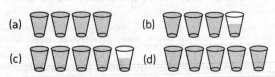

3. 50 students go to their schools by different modes as shown in the pictograph. From the pictograph, find how many students does the figure in each key represents?

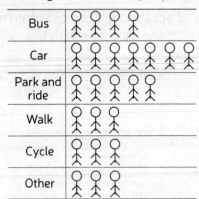

(a) 👤 = 2 students   (b) 👤 = 5 students

(c) 👤 = 10 students   (d) Cannot be determined

4. Kristine bakes muffins to sell at her cafe. The pictogram shows the number of muffins she baked on four days.

Number of cakes baked on different days

🧁 = 10 muffins   🧁 = 5 muffins

What is the total number of muffins she baked?

(a) 200   (b) 190

(c) 215   (d) None of these

Direction (Q. No. 5) The graph below shows the favourite types of literature of the students of class V (A) and class V (B). On the basis of it answer the question that follows.

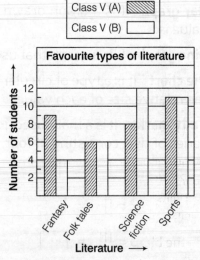

5. Which type of literature is more preferred by students in class V (A) than in class V (B) and how many students preferred the same?

(a) Sports, 9   (b) Fantasy, 5

(c) Folktales, 4   (d) Science fiction, 3

Mathematics Olympiad Class V

6. The pictograph below shows the number of orders completed by Ms. Benrick for her bakery shop.

Number of orders

Week 1	☐ ☐
Week 2	☐ ☐ ☐ ☐
Week 3	
Week 4	☐

☐ = 10 boxes

☐ = 5 boxes

If in week 3, the number of orders completed is 15 less than the number of orders completed in week 2, then which picture would depict the number of orders completed in week 3?

(a) ☐ ☐ ☐   (b) ☐ ☐ ☐

(c) ☐ ☐   (d) ☐ ☐

7. The graph below shows the length of different nails.

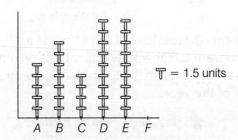

T = 1.5 units

How much longer is the nail *D* than the nail *B* ?

(a) 10.5 units   (b) 4.5 units
(c) 3 units   (d) 1 unit

8. Fill in the blanks and choose the correct option.

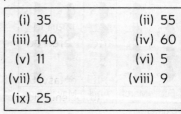

(i) 35	(ii) 55
(iii) 140	(iv) 60
(v) 11	(vi) 5
(vii) 6	(viii) 9
(ix) 25	

I. If ↓ represents 5 houses, then the number of houses represented by ↓↓↓↓ are ....

II. If one symbol △ represents 70 children the ∠ represents .... children.

III. One ☆ represents .... stars, then 12 such stars represents 72 stars.

IV. If ◇◇ represents 24 people, then......... ◇ such symbols represent 132 people.

	I	II	III	IV
(a)	(ii)	(vii)	(ix)	(v)
(b)	(ix)	(i)	(vii)	(v)
(c)	(ii)	(vi)	(iii)	(viii)
(d)	(ix)	(vii)	(iv)	(ii)

9. A tank was completely filled with water at 1 pm. To empty the tank, water was allowed to flow out at different rate. The line group below shows the volume of water in the tank from 1 pm to 4 pm.

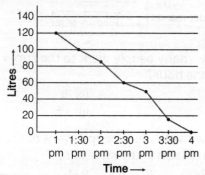

How long it take for the tank to be half-emptied?

(a) 1 hours   (b) 1.5 hours
(c) 2.5 hours   (d) 3 hours

Direction (Q. Nos. 10-11) Study the line graph given below showing the number of hours, children watch TV in a week and answer the questions that follow.

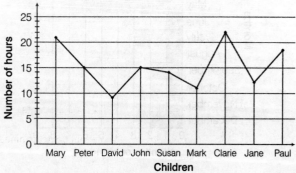

10. Who watched TV fourteen hours a week?
(a) Jane
(b) David
(c) Mark
(d) Susan

11. What is the difference between the three maximum number of hours and the three minimum number of hours of watching TV?
(a) 45 hours
(b) 32 hours
(c) 29 hours
(d) 16 hours

Direction (Q. Nos. 12-13) Kerry did a survey of the number of people who went into different shops, in one hour, in a mall. (if | means 1, ⌐ means 2, ▨ means 5 and similarly others)

Number of people who went into a shop					
Shoe shop	▨	▨	⌐		
News agent	⌐				
Post office	▨	▨	▨	▨	⌐
Bread shop	▨	▨	⌐		
Super market	▨	▨	▨	⌐	

12. How many people went to the super market in one hour?
(a) 17
(b) 18
(c) 13
(d) 3.5

13. How many more people went to the post office than in the shoe shop?
(a) 24
(b) 12
(c) 16
(d) 6

Direction (Q. Nos. 14-15) Ms. Bennet counted the number of students having birthdays in different months of the year.

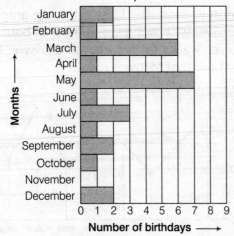

14. In how many months is the number of birthdays greater than 4?
(a) 4
(b) 3
(c) 2
(d) 1

15. How many children have birthdays during the time after 31st January and before 1st July?
(a) 18
(b) 21
(c) 16
(d) 19

Direction (Q. Nos. 16-17) This graph shows the temperature during mid day on each day in a week.

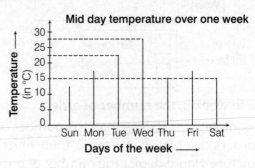

Mid day temperature over one week

16. How much higher the temperature was on Wednesday than on Saturday?
(a) 15°C
(b) 13.5°C
(c) 13°C
(d) 12.5°C

17. On which day was the temperature between 27°C and 18°C?
(a) Tuesday
(b) Monday
(c) Friday
(d) Wednesday

Direction (Q. Nos. 18-20) Tyran made a pictogram to show how many days he did not observe rainfall in his town during the first half of the year.

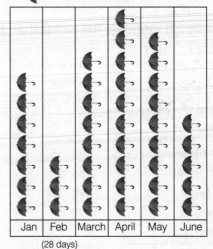

🌥⌐ = **2 Sunny days** (no rainfall)

(28 days)

18. Which month had exactly 20 rainy days?

    (a) Feb   (b) Jan

    (c) May   (d) June

19. How many sunny days were there during the first three months?

    (a) 20   (b) 26

    (c) 36   (d) 42

20. Which month had the highest number of rainy days?

    (a) January

    (b) June

    (c) February

    (d) March

21. The pictograph shows the distances of cities A, B, C and D from city E.

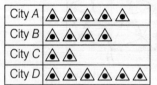

Which of the following road map shows the correct positions of cities A, B, C, D and E ?

(a)

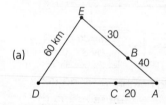

(b)

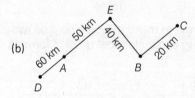

(c)

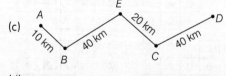

(d)

Direction (Q. Nos. 22-23) Use the pictograph, showing the number of books read by Sarah, and answer the following questions.

Number of books read by Sarah   ▢ = 2 books

May	▢ ▢ ▢ ▢ ▢ ▢ ▢ ▢
June	▢ ▢ ▢ ▢ ▢ ▢ ▢ ▢ ▢ ▢
July	▢ ▢ ▢ ▢ ▢ ▢ ▢ ▢ ▢

22. Sarah wants to add August's reading to her pictograph. She will use $11\frac{1}{2}$▢. How many books did she read in August?

    (a) 21   (b) 20   (c) 23   (d) 25

23. Suppose that the legends on scale was changed to "Each ▢ means 4 books". Then, how many books will be drawn to represent the books read in June?

    (a) $4\frac{1}{2}$ ▢   (b) 4▢

    (c) 5 ▢   (d) 10 ▢

Direction (Q. Nos. 24-25) The table given below shows the number of journey a taxi driver made on five days and the charges he took per journey (ride).

Days	Number of journeys	Money collected per ride
Monday	23	₹ 85
Tuesday	36	₹ 112
Wednesday	18	₹ 69
Thursday	31	₹ 124
Friday	35	₹ 109

24. How much money did he collect on the day when he made the most journeys?

    (a) ₹4032   (b) ₹3815

    (c) ₹4464   (d) None of these

25. How much more money did he collect on Monday than on Wednesday?

    (a) ₹ 1955   (b) ₹ 1242   (c) ₹ 713   (d) ₹ 3197

Practice Set 1

A Whole Content Based Test for Class 5th Mathematics Olympiad

1. One of the Richter puzzle is given in the figure having different types of angle formed. Which of the angle marked is an obtuse angle?

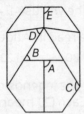

(a) A   (b) B
(c) D   (d) C

2. On the basis of arrangement given below, the value of missing number is

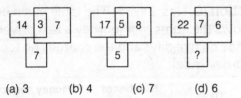

(a) 3   (b) 4   (c) 7   (d) 6

3. What is the total number of cubes in the given figure?

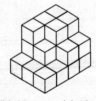

(a) 13   (b) 15   (c) 18   (d) 25

4. The line graph given below shows how the group of pupils go to office

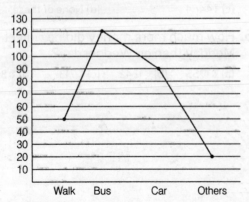

The fraction of the pupils go to office by car is

(a) $\frac{3}{28}$ (b) $\frac{9}{28}$
(c) $\frac{9}{22}$ (d) $\frac{3}{7}$

5. How many such triangles must be shaded to make AB as the line of symmetry?

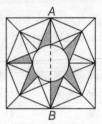

(a) 2   (b) 3
(c) 4   (d) 5

6. If

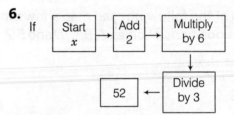

Then, the starting number is
(a) 12   (b) 18
(c) 48   (d) 36

7. Which net would make a cube where no two faces having same alphabet meet to form an edge?

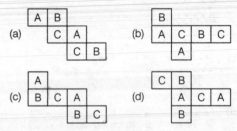

8. There was 15 kg of flour in bag A. After some flour was transferred from bag A to bag B, there was 3 kg more flour in bag A than in bag B, then there was 8 kg of flour in bag B. How much flour was transferred from bag A to bag B?
(a) 7 kg   (b) 4 kg
(c) 2 kg   (d) 11 kg

9. Jessica has 5 blue ribbons and 8 yellow ribbons. Each blue ribbon has a length of 204 cm and the total length of the ribbons Jessica has is 22.84 m. What is the length of each yellow ribbon?
(a) 124 cm (b) 196 cm (c) 208 cm (d) 158 cm

10. Study the average temperature of some major cities of India in the month of May and answer the following question based on it.

City	Average maximum temperature (in °C)	Average mimumum temperature (in °C)
New Delhi	38°	32°
Kolkata	39°	27°
Chennai	40°	28°
Mumbai	32°	28°

Which city has the least difference between its average maximum and average minimum temperature?
(a) Chennai   (b) New Delhi
(c) Mumbai   (d) Kolkata

11. How many bricks of length = 0.2 m, breadth = 0.08 m and height = 6 cm, will be needed to build a wall of length = 10 m, thickness = 0.06 m and height = 200 cm?
(a) 1250   (b) 1000   (c) 1050   (d) 900

12. The table shows the number of children in the school playground.

Playground

Children	Number
Girls	144
Boys	128

The teacher plans to arrange the children in rows having equal number of children such that, each row has either only girls or only boys.

What is the greatest number of students that could be arranged in each row?
(a) 12   (b) 16   (c) 24   (d) 32

13. Susan, Laden, John run on different tracks of a rectangular field. If the dimensions of the tracks are given below, then what is the difference between the length of boundary of track III and track I ? (neglecting the width of the back)

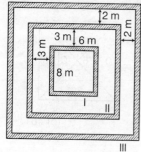

(a) 68 m   (b) 40 m
(c) 24 m   (d) 16 m

14. At 10 : 30 am, Tracy completed $\frac{5}{6}$ of her journey from town X to town Y. She had to travel another 23.9 km to reach town Y and town Z is located mid way of town X and town Y. The distance between town X and town Z is
(a) 143.4 km   (b) 28.64 km
(c) 71.7 km   (d) None of these

15. The amount of money Jack had was $\frac{2}{5}$ as much as Kerry's. After Jack received ₹ 12.40 from Kerry, Jack had $\frac{3}{4}$ as much money as Kerry. How much more money should Kerry give to Jack, so that the boys would have an equal amount of money?
(a) ₹ 54   (b) ₹ 56
(c) ₹ 68   (d) None of these

Practice Set 2

A Whole Content Based Test for Class 5th Mathematics Olympiad

1. Following the given pattern, find the value of '$C + D$'.

(a) 486
(b) 481
(c) 468
(d) None of these

2.

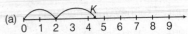

From above figure, subtracting P from 71099 and rounding off the result to the nearest thousand will give

(a) 66500   (b) 66505   (c) 67000   (d) 70000

3. Karen went running 3 times this week. Each time, she ran 2.5 mile. Which number line has point K graphed, so that it best represents the total distance (in mile) Karen ran?

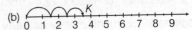

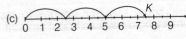

4. What is the area of the shaded part of the figure below?

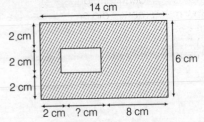

(a) 68 cm² 　(b) 72 cm² 　(c) 76 cm² 　(d) 80 cm²

5. Given,

If total weight of 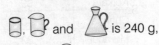 and is 240 g,

then what is the weight of ?

(a) 100 g 　(b) 110 g 　(c) 50 g 　(d) 90 g

6. Janellia has an aquarium in the shape of a cube with edges 3 cm each. She started arranging cubes with edges 1 cm each inside the aquarium in the way you can see in the picture. Atmost how many more such cubes can Janellia put into the aquarium?

(a) 9
(b) 13
(c) 17
(d) 27

7. Anita was studying the ancient number system of Aryan people. She made following table on the basis of it.

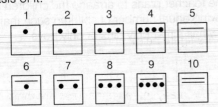

What is the symbol for 19 on the basis of above system of numbers?

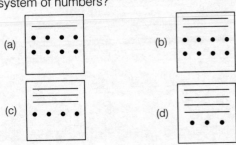

8. Boxes of height 12 inch are being stacked next to boxes that are 18 inch in height. What is the shortest height at which the two stacks of boxes will be of the same height?

(a) 2.4 inch (b) 36 inch (c) 72 inch (d) 12 inch

9.

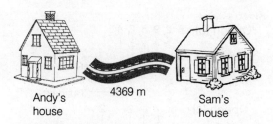

Andy's house   4369 m   Sam's house

The difference of distance between Andy's and Sam's house rounding to the nearest hundred metre and to nearest thousand metres is

(a) 200 m (b) 369 m (c) 400 m (d) 600 m

10. If $1 + 1 = 11$; $2 + 2 = 44$; $3 + 4 = 916$, then $4 + 5$ is equal to

(a) 99 (b) 1818
(c) 1625 (d) None of these

11. Four paper ribbons of uniform width 10 cm have been arranged to form Fig. (A). Each of the ribbons is 25 cm longer than the previous one. The same ribbons have been arranged to form Fig. (B). What is the difference between the perimeters of Fig. (A) and Fig. (B) ?

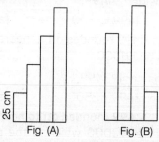

25 cm   Fig. (A)   Fig. (B)

(a) 0 cm (b) 20 cm
(c) 40 cm (d) 50 cm

12. The figure below shows a date.

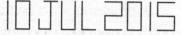

How many more right angles are there in the number than in the letters?

(a) 6 (b) 10
(c) 16 (d) 20

13.

1	2	3
4	5	6
7	8	9

Facing

Shimpy was standing on box 5. After she made a 270° turn to the right (clockwise), she faced box 4. Which number would she faced, if she had turned 135° to the left?

(a) 4
(b) 9
(c) 3
(d) 7

14. The rainfall in a city was recorded for 3 years. Study the bar graph and answer the given question.

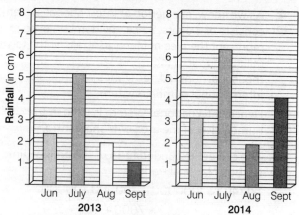

How much more rainfall was recorded in July 2014 compared to August 2013?

(a) 1.2 cm
(b) 4.4 cm
(c) 7.0 cm
(d) None of these

15. Marina used $\frac{4}{9}$ of her money to buy 9 identical blouses and 5 identical pairs of pants. She used $\frac{1}{3}$ of the remaining amount of money to buy another 10 identical blouses. She had ₹ 330 left. How much money did she have at first?

(a) ₹ 891
(b) ₹ 300
(c) ₹ 405
(d) None of the above

 # Answers *and* Solutions

① Number System

1. We have, 1 lakh = 100000
(d)   100 thousand = 100 × 1000 = 100000
    1000 hundred = 1000 × 100 = 100000
But   10 lakh = 1000000
Here, 10 lakh has one more zero than the other numbers, i.e. it is greater than the other three numbers.
So, option (d) is odd one.

2. As we know, one period of international system
(a) consists of 3 digits. Since, the number, used to represent the area of Maharashtra is of the form million, hundred thousand, ten thousand, thousand, hundred, tens, ones which is an international number system.
Hence, international system is used in the numeration of the area of Maharashtra.

3. The correct expanded form of the area of Jim
(a) Corbett National Park is
1217403 = 1000000 + 200000 + 10000
          + 7000 + 400 + 3
= 1200000 + 17000 + 400 + 3
= 12 × 100000 + 17 × 1000 + 4 × 100 + 3 × 1
= 12 lakh 17 thousand 4 hundred 3 ones

4. We have the correct expansion of
(c) 800915018 = 800000000 + 900000
          + 10000 + 5000 + <u>10</u> + 8
So, the missing number is 10.

5. We have, 19 lakh = 19 × 100000 = 1900000
(a)   19 thousand = 19 × 1000 = 19000
    19 hundred = 19 × 100 = 1900
    19 = 19 × 1 = 19
So, the correct expanded form of the number is
1900000 + 19000 + 1900 + 19 = 1920919

6. Option (a),
(c)

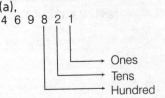

Option (b),   8 2 9 8 2 4

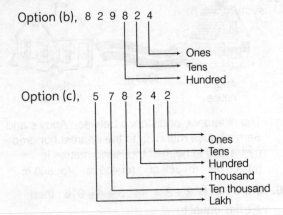

Option (c),   5 7 8 2 4 2

Here, 8 is on the thousand place.
So, 578242 is Ramia's friend's phone number.

7. (a) Consider 191400,
(c)   Here, 1400 < 1500   [as 400 < 500]
    So, 191400 rounded off to nearest thousand will be 191000.

(b) Consider 191499,
      1499 < 1500   [as 499 < 500]
    So, 191499 rounded off to nearest thousand will be 191000.

(c) Consider 192499,
    Here, 2499 < 2500   [as 499 < 500]
    So, 192499 rounded off to nearest thousand will be 192000 which is the price of bike. Therefore, 192499 is the exact price of the bike.

(d) Now, consider 192505,
      2505 > 2500   [as 505 > 500]
    So, 192505 rounded off to nearest thousand will be 193000, so it is not the exact price of the bike.
    Hence, option (c) to the correct answer.

8. We have,
(a)   5 7 9 2 4 5 6

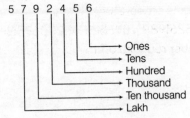

We know that 1 lakh = 100000

$$= 1 \text{ hundred thousand}$$

So, the place value of 7 in 5792456 is

7 lakh = 700000 = 7 hundred thousand

9. Writing the number according to Indian number
(c) system, we have

$$1297625 = 12,97,625$$

Here,

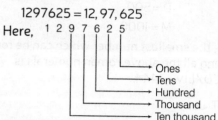

1 2 9 7 6 2 5

→ Ones
→ Tens
→ Hundred
→ Thousand
→ Ten thousand

∴ Place value of 9 = 9 × 10000

$$= 90000 (= 90 \text{ thousand})$$

and face value of 9 = 9

∴ Difference between them

$$= 90000 - 9 = 89991$$

10. We know that, the value of C = 100, D = 500,
(b) M = 1000 and L = 50

Now, CCC = 300

DC = 600 (≠ 400)

CM = 900 and CL = 150

So, option (b) is incorrectly matched.

11. Ticket number of the students are as follow:
(b)

Amaira = 392704

Samantha = 396491

Barbara = 392677

Celia = 396449

By arranging the ticket number in ascending order, we get

392677 < 392704 < 396449 < 396491

So, 396491 is the largest number

Hence, Samantha has the ticket with the largest number.

12. Number of students enrolled in various schools
(b) = 5261989

Primary school students = 1965233

High school students = 2006756

∴ Middle school students

$$= 5261989 - (1965233 + 2006756) = 1290000$$

Number rounded off to nearest lakh = 1300000

13. Rounding off each number of visitor to nearest
(d) thousand, we get

Alligator point = 13000   [as 982 > 500]

Port bella = 12000   [as 173 < 500]

St. Joe's island = 14000   [as 704 > 500]

Tucker's sound = 12000   [as 499 < 500]

So, the beach having number of visitors equal to 13000 estimated to nearest thousand is Alligator point.

14. The statements are as follow:
(b)

(a) 99999999 is the predecessor of 100000000.

(b) Let n be the number.

Successor = $n + 1$

and predecessor = $n - 1$

∴ Difference = $(n + 1) - (n - 1) = 2$

e.g. Successor and predecessor of 2 is 3 and 1, respectively.

So, difference = 3 − 1 = 2

(c) '1' is the smallest one-digit number.

(d) Face value and place value of a number are same at ones place not at all the places.

So, option (b) is correct.

15. Writing the train's number according to Indian
(c) number system, we have

14380502 = 1,43,80,502

So, we have it in words as one crore forty three lakh eighty thousand five hundred two.

16. I. 99999 < 100000
(b)

II. 9909409 < 9990409

III. 30100100 > 30100099

So, the correct sequence is <, <, >.

17. I. Commas are inserted in a number after each
(a)   <u>period</u>.

II. Place value of digit becomes <u>100</u> times as it moves from ten's place to thousand's place.

e.g. 1000 = 10 × 100

III. There is no roman number to represent <u>0</u>.

IV. 100 + 100 + 100 in roman numeral is <u>CCC</u>.

[as 100 + 100 + 100 = 300 = CCC]

18. The given digits are 7,4,0,5.
(d) Number of digits required in the number = 7

Greatest number among the given digits = 7

The greatest number formed by using 4, 0 and 5 is 540. Also, it is even.

Now, 7 is the greatest among the given digits, so it will be repeated four times to form the required 7-digit number.

∴ The required number = 7777540

19. Smallest 6-digit number = 100000
(b)
The number 10100 less than the above number
$$= 100000 - 10100 = 89900$$
Now, $42040 + \underline{\quad} = 89900$

∴ $\underline{\quad} = 89900 - 42040 = 47860$

Therefore, the required number is 47860.

20. I. $V + V = 5 + 5 = 10$
(b)
II. $XXXIV - XXVIII = 34 - 28 = 6$

III. $LI - XL = 51 - 40 = 11$

IV. $XCIX - XC = 99 - 90 = 9$

21. Number of matches held in each month is as
(b) follows
$$March = XCVI = 96$$
$$April = LXXXV = 85$$
$$May = XCIX = 99$$
$$June = XCV = 95$$
By arranging the number of matches in ascending order, we get
$$85 < 95 < 96 < 99$$
Here, 85 is the lowest number.

Therefore, in the month of April lowest number of matches were held.

22.
(c)

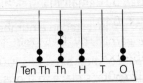

The number represented by abacus
$$= 24202$$
Now, to form a number that lies between 24631 and 25212 a ring in the thousand string must be added, i.e. 1000 must be added to 24202, we get
$$24202 + 1000 = 25202$$
$$[\text{as } 24631 < 25202 < 25212]$$

23. The value of roman numerals are as follow
(b)
$$I = 1$$
$$V = 5$$
$$X = 10$$
$$L = 50$$
$$C = 100$$
$$D = 500$$
$$M = 1000$$
So, the smallest number which can be formed using all the above roman numerals is
$$MCDXLIV = 1444.$$

24. I. True.
(c)
II. False, successor of a number is one greater than the number.

III. False, predecessor of the smallest natural number is the smallest whole number.

IV. True.

25. Place value of 1 in 100000000 is 10 crore.
(b) [as $100000000 = 10 \times 10000000 = 10$ crore]

So, the required number to be added to 3543467 to get 10 crore
$$= 100000000 - 3543467$$
$$= 96456533$$

26. Number of students who participated in
(b) National FBD English Olympiad = 6275501

Rounding off to nearest ten thousand, we get
$$6280000 \qquad [\text{as } 75501 > 75000]$$

27. Number of students participated in Science
(d) Olympiad

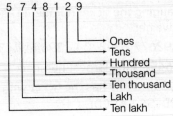

Number of students participated in English Olympiad

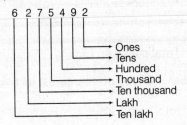

Number of students participated in Maths Olympiad

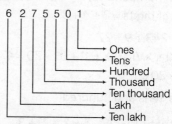

28. Rounding up 2803 gives 3000. [as 3000 > 2803]
(b)   Rounding up 3745 gives 4000.

                                    [as 4000 > 3745]

So, the estimated value will be more than the actual value of papers.

② Operations on Numbers

1. From the given numbers,
(b) we find that
(a) $479 - 277 = 202$
(b) $582 - 277 = 305$
(c) $582 - 316 = 266$
(d) $479 - 316 = 163$
Hence, option (b) is correct.

2. Option (a),
(c) $45789 \times 1 = 45789$
Option (b),
           $4579 \times 0 = 0$
Option (c),
         $45789 \times 10 = 457890$
Option (d),
         $45789 - 0 = 45789$
Hence, option (c) is incorrect.

3. Given, cost of one cupcake is ₹ 10.
(c) ∴ Cost of four cupcakes
       $= 10 + 10 + 10 + 10 = 40 = 4 \times 10$
So, multiplying 4 with the price will give the answer.

4. Since, $123456 = ABCDE \times 4$
(a) So, $ABCDE = 123456 \div 4 = 30864$
Hence, option (a) is the correct answer.

5. Number of adult tickets $= 467$
(c)   Cost of 1 ticket $= ₹ 9$
   ∴   Total cost $= 467 \times 9$
Number of youth tickets $= 215$
    Cost of 1 ticket $= ₹ 4$
So,   total cost $= 215 \times 4$

∴ Difference between the cost of adult tickets and youth tickets $= (467 \times 9) - (215 \times 4)$

6. We have,
(c) Start number $\div 45 \times 24 = 720$
So, the start number $= 720 \times 45 \div 24$
                $= \dfrac{720 \times 45}{24} = 30 \times 45$
                $= 1350$

7. The missing numbers are as follow :
(b) (i) → $50 \times 10 = 500$
   (ii) → $6 \times 7 = 42$
   (iii) → $500 + 350 = 850$
   (iv) → $60 + 42 = 102$ (or $952 - 850$)

8. Distance of the car route $= 9$ km
(d) Distance covered by car in a day
             $= 2 \times 9 = 18$ km
Now, distance covered by car in 5 days
             $= 18 \times 5 = 90$ km

9. Money earned by Benjamin in a week
(d) $= ₹ 1840$
So, money earned by Benjamin in 3 months 3 weeks $= 1840 \times 15$
      $= ₹ 27600$
[∵ number of weeks in 3 months $= 4 \times 3 = 12$,
      so total number of weeks $= 12 + 3 = 15$]

10. We find that, $495 \div 55 = 9$ hours
(b) and $396 \div 33 = 12$ hours
So, the distance travelled is 495 km and the average speed is 55 km/h.

11. Total number of sweets distributed $= 2961$
(b) Number of sweets each child received $= 3$
So, total number of children
$$= 2961 \div 3 = 987$$

12. According to the rule of operations, division is
(c) used first.
$$\therefore \quad 7 + 21 \div 3 - 8 \times 2 + 9$$
$$= 7 + 7 - 8 \times 2 + 9$$
So, the first step is $21 \div 3$.
Therefore, Sanchi did the correct step.

13. We have,
(d) Minuend $-$ Subtrahend $=$ Difference
Addend $+$ Addend $=$ Sum
Multiplicand $\times$ Multiplier $=$ Product
and Dividend $\div$ Divisor $=$ Quotient

14. We have,
(d)
$$\underline{\quad} \quad 1 \text{ (units digit)} \qquad \text{[from Step I]}$$
$$2 \times (2 \div 2) - 1 = 2 \times 1 - 1 = 2 - 1 = 1 \quad \text{[from Step II]}$$
$$3 \text{ (tens digit)} \quad \underline{1}$$
15 subtracted from 36 and then divided by 7
$$= (36 - 15) \div 7 = 21 \div 7 = 3 \qquad \text{[from Step III]}$$
So, the number is 31.

15. We know that,
(c)
$$pqrspqrs \div pqrs = 10001$$
e.g.
$$\begin{array}{r} 10001 \\ 1234 \overline{)12341234} \\ \underline{1234} \downarrow\downarrow\downarrow \\ 1234 \\ \underline{1234} \\ \times \end{array}$$

16. Given that, $A + B = C - B$
(a) which means $A + B + B = C$
$$\Rightarrow 76240 + 3245 + 3245 = C$$
$$\therefore \quad C = 82730$$

17. I. 9
(c) e.g. In number 243,
Sum of digits $= 2 + 4 + 3 = 9$
and $243 \div 9 = 27$
II. 47 (XI + XVI + XX = 11 + 16 + 20 = 47)
III. 100×20
IV. units, tens and hundred

18. Given that, $\square = 18 - 6 \times 2 + 21 \div 3$
(c) (c) Following the rule of operations, we get
$$\square = 18 - 12 + 7$$
$$[\because 21 \div 3 = 7, 6 \times 2 = 12]$$
$$= 6 + 7 = 13$$

19. Total number of people in the city $= 100000$
(d) Number of people of age below 20 $= 34768$
Numbers of people of age between 20 and 30
$$= 57498$$
So, number of people of age above 30
$$= 100000 - (34768 + 57498)$$
$$= 100000 - 92266 = 7734$$

20. Number of rows of mango trees $= 15$
(a) Number of mango trees in each row $= 325$
So, total number of mango trees $= 325 \times 15$
$$= 4875$$
Number of rows cut down $= 6$
So, number of mango trees cut down
$$= 6 \times 325 = 1950$$
Therefore, total number of mango trees left
$$= 4875 - 1950 = 2925$$

21. I. False, only 1 divisible by 1 gives quotient equal
(a) to 1.
II. True, e.g. $\dfrac{100}{10} = 10, \dfrac{1020}{10} = 102$
III. True,
$$\text{LHS} = (4 \times 6) + (4 \times 10) = 24 + 40 = 64$$
$$\text{RHS} = 4 \times (6 + 10) = 4 \times 16 = 64$$
So, $\text{LHS} = \text{RHS}$
IV. True (by definition)

22. Given,
(c)

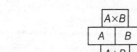

$$\triangle + \triangle + \square = 255$$

and

$$\triangle - \square = 30$$

So,

$$\triangle - 30 = \square$$

Therefore,

$$\triangle + \triangle + \triangle - 30 = 255$$

$$\Rightarrow \quad 3\triangle = 255 + 30 = 285$$

$$\therefore \quad \triangle = 95$$

23. We have the following operations :
(c)

$A \times B$	
A	B
$A + B$	

So, we have

350	$\rightarrow 14 \times 25$		(ii) 774	$\rightarrow 43 \times 18$
(i) 14	25		43	(iii) 18 $\rightarrow 61 - 43$
39			61	

14 + 25

(i) $\rightarrow 14$,   (ii) $\rightarrow 774$,   (iii) $\rightarrow 18$

24. Here, collection made by each class is as follows :
(a)
Class 1 = 728 × 25 = 18200

Class 2 = 225 × 40 = 9000

Class 3 = 374 × 20 = 7480

and Class 4 = 280 × 30 = 8400

Here, 18200 is the greatest number.

So, class 1 collected the maximum number of food items.

25. Number of packets collected by class 1
(c)
$$= 728 \times 25 = 18200$$

If class 2 has to collect 18200 packets in 40 days, then the number of packets it must collect each day = 18200 ÷ 40 = 455

3 Factors and Multiples

1. Here,
(b)
HCF (22, 33) = 11   [∵ 22 = 2 × 11 and 33 = 3 × 11]

HCF (20, ?) = 5

So, the missing number is 15.

[as HCF (20, 15) = 5, where 20 = 5 × 4

and 15 = 5 × 3]

2. Annie's score → lowest multiple of 10 = 10
(a)
Jass's score → fourth multiple of 3 = 12 (3 × 4)

Krish's score → highest factor of 15 = 15

By arranging the scores in ascending order, we get 15 < 12 < 10

So, Annie < Jass < Krish.

3. We have,
(c)
Multiples of 2 = 2, 4, 6, 8, 10, 12, 14, 16, 18, ...

Multiples of 4 = 4, 8, 12, 16, 20, ...

Multiples of 8 = 8, 16, 24, ...

So,

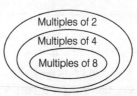

Therefore, Jimmy had drawn the correct picture.

4. In other options the second number is divisible
(d) by the first number except in option (d) as

1111 ÷ 11 = 101,   444 ÷ 4 = 111,   1717 ÷ 17 = 101

But 999 is not exactly divisible by 99.

5. I. Prime, composite
(b)
II. Twin primes   [by definition]

III. Factor, multiple

IV. LCM × HCF

e.g. LCM of 2 and 3 = 6

HCF of 2 and 3 = 1

∴ Product of 2 and 3 = 6

= LCM of 2 and 3 × HCF of 2 and 3

6.
(c) Here, the angles drawn are of measure 50°, 80°, 110°, 140°.

Now, HCF (50°, 80°, 110°, 140°) = 10°

[as 50 = 5 × 5 × 2, 80 = 2 × 2 × 2 × 2 × 5,

110 = 2 × 5 × 11, 140 = 2 × 2 × 5 × 7]

Now, LCM (2°, 5°) = 10° and HCF (10°, 100°) = 10°

Hence, both are equivalent to relation of the given angles.

7.
(b) Book A is read on every fourth day.

Book B is read on every fifth day.

Book C is read on every sixth day.

So, the day when all the books will be read together

= LCM (4, 5, 6) = 60 th day

[as 4 = 2 × 2, 5 = 5 × 1, 6 = 2 × 3

and LCM (4, 5, 6) = 2 × 2 × 3 × 5]

8.
(c) LCM of above two numbers = HCF of below two numbers, i.e. LCM (2, 3) = 6

HCF (12, 30) = 6

Now, HCF of (36, 60) = 12

LCM of (4, ?) = 12 = 2 × 2 × 3

So, from the given options, $x = 6$

9.
(c) Visit in which Saran receives a free beverage = 9th

Visit in which she receives a free appetiser = 12th

Visit in which Saran receives both a free beverage and a free appetiser

= LCM (9, 12) = 36th

[as 9 = 3 × 3, 12 = 2 × 2 × 3, so

LCM (9, 12) = 2 × 2 × 3 × 3 = 36]

10.
(c) HCF (75, 225) = 75

As, 75 = 1 × 5 × 5 × 3

and 225 = 1 × 5 × 5 × 3 × 3

So, HCF (75, 225) = 5 × 5 × 3

Also, every even number is divisible by 2.

Thus, 2 is a factor of every even number.

Hence, both Robin and Robert are correct.

11.
(c) We have the factor tree of 90 is as follows

So, option (c) is correct.

12.
(b) LCM (2, 5, 6) = 5 × 6 = 30

Smallest value of X = 30

LCM (4, 8) = 8

[as 4 = 2 × 2 and 8 = 2 × 2 × 2,

so LCM (4, 8) = 2 × 2 × 2 = 8]

Smallest value of Y = 8

13.
(b) We have factor tree of 150 is as follows

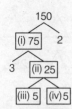

So, (i) → 75, (ii) → 25, (iii) → 5 and (iv) → 5

14.
(d) The contents are to be packed separately in the packets of same weight.

So, the maximum weight of each packet

= HCF (8, 16, 4, 14) = 2 oz

[as 8 = 2 × 2 × 2, 16 = 2 × 2 × 2 × 2,

4 = 2 × 2, 14 = 2 × 7,

so HCF (8, 16, 4, 14) = 2]

15.
(d) The perimeter of the larger sheet

= LCM (3, 4, 5) = 3 × 2 × 2 × 5 = 60 units

As,

3	3, 4, 5
2	1, 4, 5
2	1, 2, 5
5	1, 1, 5
	1, 1, 1

16.
(b) I. Given, HCF of numbers = 2

and LCM of numbers = 60

So, product of numbers = 60 × 2 = 120

and 120 = (2 × 60), (3 × 40),

(4 × 30), (5 × 24),

(6 × 20), (8 × 15), $\boxed{(10 × 12)}$

Also, HCF of numbers = 3

and LCM of numbers = 90

∴ Product of numbers = 3 × 90 = 270

and 270 = (2 × 135), (3 × 90), (5 × 54), (6 × 45),

(9 × 30), (10 × 27), (15 × 18)

So, there are more than three such pairs.

Hence, Luke is correct.

17. I. Odd numbers
(d) II. Composite numbers
III. Even numbers
IV. Prime numbers

18. Multiple of $6 = 6, 12, 18, 24, 30, 36, 42, 48, 54, 60$
(c) These all are even numbers. They have 6, 2, 8, 4, 0 as the unit digit.
Since, 6, 18, 30,... are not divisible by 12.
These all are divisible by 3.
So, Chrish is correct.

19. Number of onions $= 56 = 2 \times 2 \times 2 \times 7$
(b) Number of potatoes $= 32 = 2 \times 2 \times 2 \times 2 \times 2$
Number of tomatoes $= 64$
$$= 2 \times 2 \times 2 \times 2 \times 2 \times 2$$
The maximum number of vegetables of same type he can keep in each basket
$$= \text{HCF}(56, 32, 64) = 2 \times 2 \times 2 = 8$$

20. Number of onions $= 56$
(a) Number of potatoes $= 32$
Number of tomatoes $= 64$
$$\text{HCF}(56, 32, 64) = 8$$
[as in the above question]
Number of baskets of onions $= \dfrac{56}{8} = 7$
Number of baskets of potatoes $= \dfrac{32}{8} = 4$
Number of baskets of tomatoes $= \dfrac{64}{8} = 8$

21. For Reenu's statement,
(d) Consider $X = 14$ and $Y = 15$
$\text{HCF}(14, 15) = 1$
For Reshma's statement,
Consider $X = 2$ and $Y = 4$
$$\text{HCF}(2, 4) = 2$$
Also, $4 \div 2 = 2$
For Karuna's statement,
Consider $X = 2$, $Y = 3$ and $Z = 4$

Now, $\text{HCF}(X, Y) = \text{HCF}(2, 3) = 1$
$\text{HCF}(Y, Z) = \text{HCF}(3, 4) = 1$
But $\text{HCF}(X, Z) = \text{HCF}(2, 4) = 2$
For Suparna's statement,
Consider $X = 14$ and $Y = 15$
Now, $X + 1 = Y \Rightarrow 14 + 1 = 15 \Rightarrow 15 = 15$

Hence, except Karuna all others have said the correct statement.

22. Margret went for singing class on every 3rd day,
(b) dancing class on every 4th day and drawing class on every 6th day.
The day on which she will go for all her classes $= \text{LCM}(3, 4, 6) = 12$th
The day on which she went for all the three classes before $= 5$th, Monday
So, the next time she will go for all the three classes on the same day $= 5 + 12 = 17$th, Saturday

23. I. True, 1 is a factor of even number.
(d) II. True, 0 is neither a prime number nor a composite number.
III. False, LCM of two number $\times$ HCF of two numbers $=$ Product of two numbers
IV. False, HCF of two coprime numbers $= 1$

24. We have, $80 = 2 \times 2 \times 2 \times 2 \times 5$
(a) $110 = 2 \times 5 \times 11$
$\therefore \text{HCF}(80, 110) = 2 \times 5$
So, the common area $= \text{HCF}(80, 110) = 2 \times 5$

25. The time when water in all the colours will be
(c) erected out from the fountain
$$= \text{LCM}(40, 50, 60)$$
[as $40 = 2 \times 2 \times 2 \times 5, 60 = 2 \times 2 \times 3 \times 5$
$50 = 2 \times 5 \times 5$,
so $\text{LCM} = 2 \times 2 \times 2 \times 3 \times 5 \times 5 = 600$]
$$= 600 \text{ minutes}$$
$$= 10 \text{ hours}$$
So, after 8 am the water in all colours will be erected at 6 pm.

4 Fractions

1.
(c)

Part of cake left for Greg's friends $=\dfrac{1}{2}+\dfrac{1}{4}=\dfrac{3}{4}$

∴ Part of cake eaten by Greg $=1-\dfrac{3}{4}=\dfrac{1}{4}$

2.
(b)

Duration of time, Tom talked to Hary $=\dfrac{1}{6}$ hour

Duration of time, Tom talked to Geet $=\dfrac{5}{3}$ hours

Duration of time, Tom talked to Ryan $=\dfrac{1}{4}$ hour

Total time spent on the telephone by Tom

$=\dfrac{1}{6}+\dfrac{5}{3}+\dfrac{1}{4}$

$=\dfrac{2+20+3}{12}$

[by taking LCM $(6, 3, 4)=2\times2\times3=12$]

$=\dfrac{25}{12}=2\dfrac{1}{12}$ hours

3.
(a)

We have the simplest form as

$\dfrac{3}{15}=\dfrac{1}{5}$, $\dfrac{16}{31}=\dfrac{16}{31}$

$\dfrac{9}{17}=\dfrac{9}{17}$ and $\dfrac{4}{5}=\dfrac{4}{5}$

So, $\dfrac{3}{15}$ is incorrect as it is not in the correct simplest form while all others are in the simplest form.

4.
(b)

Number of shaded parts $=9$

Total number of parts $=13$

Here, two more parts can be drawn.

So, total number of parts in the figure

$=13+2=15$

Now, $\dfrac{2}{3}\times$ Total parts $=\dfrac{2}{3}\times15=10$

So, the more number of shaded parts should be
$=10-9=1$

Remaining parts (not to be shaded) $=2-1=1$

∴ Number of unshaded part to be added $=1$

5.
(b)

Total number of shapes $=6\times4=24$

Number of stars drawn $=8$

∴ The part of picture which are having stars
$=\dfrac{8}{24}=\dfrac{1}{3}$

6.
(c)

Part of the class assignment coloured by Florence

$=1+1+1+1+\dfrac{3}{7}=4+\dfrac{3}{7}$

$=\dfrac{28+3}{7}=\dfrac{31}{7}=4\dfrac{3}{7}$

So, marks obtained by Florence $=4\dfrac{3}{7}$

7.
(c)

Here, $1\dfrac{9}{10}=1+\dfrac{9}{10}=\dfrac{19}{10}$

Now, $\dfrac{10}{10}<\dfrac{19}{10}<\dfrac{20}{10}$

i.e. $1<\dfrac{19}{10}<2$

Dividing the part on scale between 1 and 2 in 10 equal parts

So, point C represents $\dfrac{19}{10}=1\dfrac{9}{10}$.

8.
(d)

Number of triangles having holes $=9$

Number of triangles having odd number of holes $=6$

So, the required fraction $=\dfrac{6}{9}=\dfrac{2}{3}$

9.
(d)

Number of weeks of summer vacation $=12$

Number of songs learnt in 12 weeks $=6$

So, song learnt every week $=\dfrac{6}{12}=\dfrac{1}{2}$ of a song

10.
(b)

In option (a),

Number of pies each one got $=\dfrac{24}{8}\neq\dfrac{8}{24}$

In option (b),

Part of day when Grimmy sleeps $=\dfrac{8}{24}=\dfrac{8}{24}$

In option (c),

Number of bananas in each shake

$=\dfrac{2\times12}{8}=\dfrac{24}{8}\neq\dfrac{8}{24}$

In option (d),

Number of toys received by each group

$=\dfrac{24}{8}\neq\dfrac{8}{24}$

11. Total money saved by the six friends
(a)
$$= ₹210 + ₹300 + ₹50 + ₹100 + ₹95 + ₹245$$
$$= ₹1000$$

Now, $\dfrac{1}{20}$ th part of the whole amount

$$= \dfrac{1}{20} \times 1000 = ₹50$$

Here, Kim saved $₹50 = \dfrac{1}{20}$ th part of the whole amount

Hence, option (a) is correct.

12. Total number of square boxes = 16
(b)
Number of boxes coloured red = 4

∴ Fraction of boxes coloured red $= \dfrac{4}{16} = \dfrac{1}{4}$

Number of boxes coloured green

$$= 1 + \dfrac{1}{2} + \dfrac{1}{2} = 2$$

So, fraction of boxes which are coloured green

$$= \dfrac{2}{16} = \dfrac{1}{8}$$

Number of boxes coloured blue = 1

So, required fraction $= \dfrac{1}{16}$

Number of boxes coloured black = 3

So, required fraction is $\dfrac{3}{16}$.

∴ I → (iii)   II → (i)

   III → (ii)   IV → (iv)

Hence, option (b) is correct.

13. We have,
(c)
$$\dfrac{7}{9} \times \dfrac{4}{4} = \dfrac{28}{36} \text{ or } \dfrac{28}{34} \div \dfrac{4}{4} = \dfrac{7}{9}$$

Similarly,

$$\dfrac{12}{20} = \dfrac{3}{5} \times \dfrac{4}{4} \text{ and } \dfrac{16}{28} = \dfrac{4}{7} \times \dfrac{4}{4}$$

So, group A is obtained by multiplying the numerator and denominator of group B by 4.

14. As each slice is $\dfrac{1}{6}$ th of the pizza.
(d)
So, number of pizza slice in one pizza = 6

Total pizzas = 4

So, total number of pizza slices $= 6 \times 4 = 24$

Number of slice each one of 8 people gets $= \dfrac{24}{8} = 3$

15. Time taken by Jinny to walk to the playground
(c)
$$= \dfrac{5}{6} \text{ hour}$$

Time taken by Jinny to walk from the playground to school $= \dfrac{1}{4}$ hour

So, time taken by Jinny to walk to the playground and then to school

$$= \dfrac{5}{6} + \dfrac{1}{4} = \dfrac{10+3}{12} = \dfrac{13}{12} = 1\dfrac{1}{12} \text{ hours}$$

16. Compare the scores obtained by each player.
(c)
$$\dfrac{75}{100}, \dfrac{46}{50}, \dfrac{54}{60}, \dfrac{72}{100}, \dfrac{89}{100}$$

Converting them to equivalent fraction by multiply the numerator and denominator by a common number.

By taking LCM and converting them into equivalent fraction, we get

$$\dfrac{225}{300}, \dfrac{276}{300}, \dfrac{270}{300}, \dfrac{216}{300}, \dfrac{267}{300}$$

$$[\because \text{LCM } (100, 50, 60) = 300]$$

On arranging the numerator in descending order, we get

$$276 > 270 > 267 > 225 > 216$$

$$[\text{since, denominator are equal}]$$

Therefore, we get

$$\text{Shim} > \text{Rose} > \text{Den} > \text{Ken} > \text{Jack}$$

Hence, Shim scored the highest.

17. Highest score (of Shim) $= \dfrac{46}{50}$
(a)
and lowest score (of Jack) $= \dfrac{72}{100}$

∴ Difference between their scores $= \dfrac{46}{50} - \dfrac{72}{100}$

$$= \dfrac{92}{100} - \dfrac{72}{100} = \dfrac{20}{100} = \dfrac{1}{5}$$

18. We have, 3 cups = 1 jar
(b)
So, $\dfrac{1}{2}$ jar $= \dfrac{3}{2}$ cups

To pour the juice that fills the jar half full, number of cups required $= \dfrac{3}{2}$ cups

Now, cups of orange juice poured $= \dfrac{1}{2}$ cup

So, total number of cups of juice poured

$$= \dfrac{3}{2} + \dfrac{1}{2} = \dfrac{4}{2} = 2 \text{ cups}$$

Now, amount of jar filled by 3 cups $= 1$

So, amount of jar filled by 1 cup $= \dfrac{1}{3}$

Therefore, amount of jar filled by 2 cups

$= \dfrac{2}{3}$ or two-third

19. Distance to which Victor can
(c) kick the football $= 7\dfrac{5}{7}$ ft $= \dfrac{54}{7}$ ft

Distance to which Leon can
kick the same football $= 10\dfrac{4}{5}$ ft $= \dfrac{54}{5}$ ft

Therefore, the number of times the height to which Victor kicks the ball as compared to Leon

$= \dfrac{54}{7} \div \dfrac{54}{5} = \dfrac{54}{7} \times \dfrac{5}{54} = \dfrac{5}{7}$

20. I. Improper, since $16 > 13$
(d)   i.e. numerator $>$ denominator

II. $\dfrac{5}{4}$

III. Unlike

IV. 1, e.g. $\dfrac{5}{6} \times \dfrac{6}{5} = 1$

21. Here, shaded part in Fig. I $= 1 + \dfrac{10}{12}$
(a)

$= 1 + \dfrac{5}{6} = 1\dfrac{5}{6} = \dfrac{11}{6}$

and shaded part in Fig. II $= 1 + \dfrac{12}{20} = 1 + \dfrac{3}{5} = 1\dfrac{3}{5} = \dfrac{8}{5}$

Now, on comparing $\dfrac{11}{6}$ and $\dfrac{8}{5}$, we get

$\dfrac{55}{30}, \dfrac{30}{30}$

[by converting them into equivalent fractions]

$\therefore$ $\dfrac{11}{6} > \dfrac{8}{5}$ $[\because 55 > 30]$

So,   Fig. I $>$ Fig. II

22. Number of coins the prince had $= 35$
(b)
Part of coins given to gatekeeper $= \dfrac{2}{5}$

Remaining part of coins $= 1 - \dfrac{2}{5} = \dfrac{3}{5}$

So, number of coins left with the prince

$= \dfrac{3}{5}$ of total coins

$= \dfrac{3}{5} \times 35 = 21$

23. I. True, $2 \times \dfrac{1}{5} = \dfrac{2}{1} \times \dfrac{1}{5} = \dfrac{2}{5}$
(c)
II. False, $15 \times \dfrac{1}{10} = \dfrac{15}{10} = \dfrac{3}{2}$

III. True, $1 + 1 + 1 + \dfrac{1}{2} = 3\dfrac{1}{2}$

IV. False,

$\dfrac{2}{3}$ and $\dfrac{4}{6}$ are proper fractions as numerator is smaller than denominator.

24. Total number of hours worked in a week $= 15$
(c) Number of hours worked on Monday

$= 3\dfrac{1}{2} = \dfrac{7}{2}$

Number of hours worked on Tuesday $= 4$

Number of hours worked on Wednesday

$= 2\dfrac{1}{6} = \dfrac{13}{6}$

Number of hours worked on Thursday

$= 1\dfrac{1}{2} = \dfrac{3}{2}$

So, total number of hours worked in four days

$= \dfrac{7}{2} + 4 + \dfrac{13}{6} + \dfrac{3}{2}$

$= \dfrac{21 + 24 + 13 + 9}{6} = \dfrac{67}{6}$

So, number of hours worked on Friday

$=$ Total number of hours worked in a week
      $-$ Total number of hours worked in four days

$= 15 - \dfrac{67}{6} = \dfrac{90 - 67}{6}$

$= \dfrac{23}{6} = 3\dfrac{5}{6}$ hours

25. Jessica's square shows the fraction $= \dfrac{2}{8} = \dfrac{1}{4}$
(b)

and Denmark's square shows the fraction

$= \dfrac{4}{8} = \dfrac{1}{2}$

Now, option (b) represents $\dfrac{2}{5}$.

On comparing $\dfrac{2}{5}, \dfrac{1}{2}$ and $\dfrac{1}{4}$ by converting them

into equivalent fractions, we get

$\dfrac{8}{20}, \dfrac{10}{20}, \dfrac{5}{20},$ so $\dfrac{5}{20} < \dfrac{8}{20} < \dfrac{10}{20}$

$\therefore$ $\dfrac{2}{5} < \dfrac{1}{2}$ but $\dfrac{2}{5} > \dfrac{1}{4}$

Hence, option (b) will be Andrew's square.

5 Decimals

1.
(d) Total amount of wheat $= 236\,$kg

$\therefore$ Amount of wheat 1 person will get $= \dfrac{236}{16}$

On dividing,

$$16)\overline{236}(14.75$$
$$\underline{16\downarrow}$$
$$76$$
$$\underline{64}$$
$$120$$
$$\underline{112}$$
$$80$$
$$\underline{80}$$
$$\times$$

So, each one will get 14.75 kg of wheat.

2.
(a) Given, $A = 31.36$ and $B = 45.63$

$\therefore \quad 2A - B = 2 \times 31.36 - 45.63$

$\qquad\qquad = 62.72 - 45.63 = 17.09$

3.
(a) We have the sequence of jumps made by the five children in descending order as

$4.50 > 4.28 > 4.06 > 3.99 > 3.09$

So, Alex won the long jump competition.

4.
(b) Number of squares shaded $= 29$

Since, each $\square = 0.02$

So, decimal represent by the shaded squares
$$= 29 \times 0.02 = 0.58$$

5.
(c) The given number is as follows :

$3 \times 1000 + 5 \times 100 + 0 \times 10 + 11 \times 1$

$\qquad + \dfrac{0}{10} + \dfrac{3}{100} + \dfrac{5}{1000}$

$= 3000 + 500 + 11 + \dfrac{3}{100} + \dfrac{5}{1000} = 3511.035$

6.
(a) The given numbers when rounded off to two decimal places will be equal to

$\quad 4.123 \longrightarrow 4.12 \qquad [\because 3 < 5]$

$\quad 7.299 \longrightarrow 7.30 \qquad [\because 9 > 5]$

$\quad 14.756 \longrightarrow 14.76 \qquad [\because 6 > 5]$

$\quad 0.014 \longrightarrow 0.01 \qquad [\because 4 < 5]$

7.
(b) The correct ascending order of the sugar bags according to their weight is

$\quad 6.08 < 6.10 < 6.18 < 6.80 < 6.81$

8.
(b) Total cost of a pair of jeans, a black shirt and a bag from shop 1

$\quad = ₹\,1147.21 + ₹\,534.23 + ₹\,520.12 = ₹\,2201.56$

Total cost of pair of jeans, a black shirt and a bag from shop 2

$\quad = ₹\,1272.46 + ₹\,324.49 + ₹\,420.41 = ₹\,2017.36$

Total cost of pair of jeans, a black shirt and a bag from shop 3

$\quad = ₹\,1014.76 + ₹\,576.23 + ₹\,500.29 = ₹\,2091.28$

Arranging the cost in descending order, we get

$\quad 2201.56 > 2091.28 > 2017.36$

The total cost is least from shop 2, so she should buy the items from shop 2.

9.
(c) Present height of Andrew $+ 35\,$cm $= 2.5\,$m

So, present height of Andrew

$\quad = 2.5\,$m $- 35\,$cm

$\quad = 2.5\,$m $- 0.35\,$m $\qquad \left[\because 1\,cm = \dfrac{1}{100}m\right]$

$\quad = 2.15\,$m

$\therefore$ Andrew's present height $= 2.15\,$m

10.
(a) A shown by the below number line

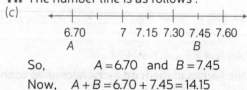

Number on left side are smaller and number on right side are greater, so Minti said the correct statement.

11.
(c) The number line is as follows :

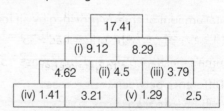

So, $A = 6.70$ and $B = 7.45$

Now, $A + B = 6.70 + 7.45 = 14.15$

12.
(c) The complete figure is as follows :

	17.41			
	(i) 9.12	8.29		
	4.62	(ii) 4.5	(iii) 3.79	
(iv) 1.41	3.21	(v) 1.29	2.5	

Here, (i) $= 17.41 - 8.29 = 9.12$

$\quad$ (ii) $= 9.12 - 4.62 = 4.5$

$\quad$ (iii) $= 8.29 - 4.5 = 3.79$

$\quad$ (iv) $= 4.62 - 3.21 = 1.41$

$\quad$ (v) $= 4.5 - 3.21 = 1.29$

13. I. True, 15.73 = 15.7 (as 3 < 5)
(a)
   II. False, 6 hundredth is written as 0.06.

   III. False, digit 5 in 24.56 stands for 5 tenth.

   IV. False, 0.023 lies between 0.02 and 0.03.

14. Paint left in each paint pot is as follows :
(a)
   (i) 1.2 L   (ii) 1.09 L

   (iii) 0.99 L   (iv) 0.10 L

   So, the total quantity of paint left

   = 1.2 L + 1.09 L + 0.99 L + 0.10 L = 3.38 L

15. Quantity of paint used from each paint pot is as
(b) follows :

   I. 2 − 1.2 L = 0.8 L

   II. 2 − 1.09 L = 0.91 L

   III. 2 − 0.99 L = 1.01 L

   IV. 2 − 0.10 L = 1.9 L

   So, the difference between the maximum and minimum quantity of paint used

   = 1.9 L − 0.8 L = 1.1 L

16. I. The fraction $\dfrac{6}{25}$ is equal to decimal number 0.24.
(d)
   II. 15.8 − 6.73 = 9.07

   III. 9.07 rounded off nearest tenth is 9.1 as 7 > 5, so 9.07 = 9.1 when rounded off to nearest tenth.

   IV. 9.0 (as 0.037 < 0.050)

17. Ascending order of the energy provided by each
(b) food item is

   4.09 < 4.25 < 4.31 < 4.72

   So, the names of the food items according to the above ascending order is

   Milk < Wheat < Rice < Potatoes

18. Total amount of energy provided by all food
(c) items = 4.25 J + 4.31 J + 4.72 J + 4.09 J = 17.37 J

19. Emma's mass = 4.65 kg and Zua's mass = 5.25 kg
(b)
   ∴ Difference between their masses

   = (5.25 − 4.65) kg

   = 0.60 kg or 600 g   [∵ 1 kg = 1000 g]

20. Joy's mass = 3.75 kg
(d) and Luca's mass = 4.96 kg

   ∴ Total mass = (3.75 + 4.96) kg = 8.71 kg

21. Brian's pocket money = 15 pounds
(d)
   Brian's pocket money in Indian rupees

   = 15 × 93.75 = ₹ 1406.25

   Money transferred to friend = ₹ 375.50

   Therefore, money left with Brian

   = 1406.25 − 375.50 = ₹ 1030.75

22. Age of youngest sister of Tyran = 9 years
(c)
   ∴ Age of Tyran = 9 + 9 = 18 years

   Cost of tickets for adults = ₹ 6.00

   Cost of tickets for children = ₹ 3.75

   So, cost of tickets for Tyran's sisters

   = 2 × 3.75 = ₹ 7.5

   So, total money spent

   = ₹ 6.00 + ₹ 7.5

   = ₹ 13.5

23. Cost of tickets for parents = 2 × 6 = ₹ 12
(a)
   So, total cost of tickets of all five members of family = ₹ 13.5 + ₹ 12

   = ₹ 25.5

   Total cost of snacks

   = ₹ 2.75 + ₹ 4.35 = ₹ 7.1

   So, total money spent by the family

   = ₹ 7.1 + ₹ 25.5 = ₹ 32.6

24. Hourwise charges on Monday
(a)
   10 am to 11 am = 1 × ₹ 1.50 = ₹ 1.50 (1 hour)

   11 am to 5 pm = 6 × ₹ 2.20 = ₹ 13.2 (6 hours)

   5 pm to 6 : 50 pm = 4 × ₹ 0.50 = ₹ 2

                              (approx 4 half hour)

   Total charges on Monday

   = ₹ (1.50 + 13.2 + 2) = ₹ 16.7

25. Hourwise charges for Sunday
(b)
   10 am to 11 am = 1 × ₹ 1.20 = ₹ 1.20 (1 hour)

   11 am to 5 pm = 6 × ₹ 1.80 = ₹ 10.8 (6 hours)

   5 pm to 6.50 pm = 4 × ₹ 2.20

                       = ₹ 8.8 (approx 4 half hour)

   Total charges on Sunday = ₹ (1.20 + 10.8 + 8.8)

                       = ₹ 20.8

   ∴ Difference between the charges on Sunday and Monday

   = ₹ 20.8 − ₹ 16.7

   [from above question, total charge on Monday]

   = ₹ 4.1

⑥ Geometry

1.
(b) Only option figure (b) is open as its starting point and its end point do not coincide, whereas other figures are closed.

2.
(a) The angle formed by the arrow with the ground has measure greater than 90°, so it makes an obtuse angle with the ground.

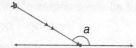

3.
(d) The angle formed in figure (d) measures 90°, whereas the angles formed in other figures have measure greater than 90°, i.e. obtuse angles.

4.
(d) Measure of angle in option (a) is less than 90°, so it is an acute angle. Measure of angle in option (b) is equal to 90°, so it is a right angle. Measure of angle in option (c) is greater than 90°, so it is an obtuse angle. Measure of angle in option (d) is greater than 90°, so it is an obtuse angle.

Therefore, option (d) is correctly matched while others are not correctly matched.

5.
(c) The measure of angles a, b and d is less than 90° but that of angle c is greater than 90°, so angle c is an obtuse angle.

6.
(c) Number of right angles formed in Fig. I = 0
[since, none of the angle is of 90° in the given figure]
Number of right angles formed in Fig. II = 2

Number of right angles formed in Fig. III = 1

So, on comparing, we get II > III > I.

7.
(b) Angle c formed by the rods of the stretcher has measure greater than 90°, so it is an obtuse angle whereas angle a, angle b and angle d are acute angles.

8.
(c) All shapes have equal number of sides but the angles formed are different. So, Kandy said the correct statement.

9.
(a) The letters making acute angles are as follow :

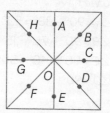

So, there are nine acute angles.

10.
(c)

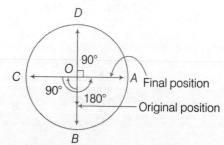

Here, the number of right angles formed are AOC, BOD, COE, DOF, EOG, FOH, GOA, HOB.
So, total number of right angles formed = 8

11.
(d) In question figure, all three angles are making an acute angle as their measures are less than 90°.

12.
(b) The measure of angles formed in a polygon is
P → less than 90° → Acute angle
Q → equal to 90° → Right angle
R → greater than 90° → Obtuse angle
S → greater than 90° → Obtuse angle
T → equal to 180° → Straight angle

13.
(b)

While turning 90° clockwise, the hour hand rests at OC and then turning 180° anti-clockwise, it rests at OA, hence ∠DOA = 90°

Thus, the angle formed by the minute and hour hands of the clock after rotation is 90°.

14.
(d) I. ∵ Right angle = 90°
∴ $\frac{1}{2}$ right angle = $\frac{90°}{2}$ = 45°

II. ∵ Complete turn = 360°
∴ $\frac{3}{4}$ turn = $\frac{3}{4}$ × 360° = 270°

III. 90°, it will form a right angle.

IV. ∠ABC = ∠ABD + ∠DBE + ∠EBC

$\Rightarrow$ 90° = 17° + ∠DBE + 32°

$\Rightarrow$ 90 = 49° + ∠DBE

∴   ∠DBE = 90° − 49° = 41°

15. Since, Sindri likes his web angles to be a perfect
(d) 90° angle, so we have

In Fig. I,   ∠A = 90° − 38° = 52°

In Fig. II,   ∠B = 90° − 75° = 15°

In Fig. III,   ∠C = 90° − 40° = 50°

In Fig. IV,   ∠D = 90°

16. ∠B = 90°   [given]
(d) Sum of the angles of a triangle = 180°

i.e. ∠A + ∠B + ∠C = 180°

So, the sum of the measure of other two angles,

i.e.   ∠A + ∠C = 180° − 90° = 90°

17. I. True, e.g. Rectangle ▭ and square ☐
(d)
II. True,

because ⌐

III. True, both have 90° angles

IV. True

∵ Complete turn = 360°

∴ $\dfrac{1}{4}$ turn $= \dfrac{360°}{4} = 90°$

18.
(b)

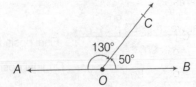

By using protractor we see that, with base OB,
the angle formed is of measure 50°, but with
base OA the same angle is of measure 130°.

19. In slide I,   ∠B = 90°, ∠A = 20°, ∠C = a
(c) We have,   ∠A + ∠B + ∠C = 180°

[since, sum of angles of a triangle = 180°]

∠C = 180° − ∠B − ∠A

∴   = 180° − 90° − 20°

$\Rightarrow$ ∠C = 90° − 20° = 70°

In slide II,   ∠B′ = 90°, ∠A′ = 35°, ∠C′ = b

We have,   ∠A′ + ∠B′ + ∠C′ = 180°

∠C′ = 180° − ∠B′ − ∠A′

     = 180° − 90° − 35°

$\Rightarrow$ ∠C′ = 90° − 35° = 55°

20. In clock I, the angle made between the hands
(b)   = 180° − 35° − 55°

[∵ sum of all three angles of a triangle is 180°]

           = 180° − 90° = 90°

In clock II, the angle made between the hands is
greater than 90°.

So,   ∠O = 180° − (75° + 40°)

          = 180° − 115° = 65°

In clock III, the angle made between the hands

          = 180° − (35° + 20°)

          = 180° − 55° = 125°

In clock IV, the angle made between the hands

          = 180° − (45° + 25°)

          = 180° − 70° = 110°

21. First score of Michael = 4
(a) Score required to win = 18 − 4 = 14

At any angle less than 90°, he will not score
exactly 14 points.

At any angle less than 170°, he can get a score
less than 14, so his win is not sure.

At any angle between 135° to 116°, he will get a
score of 12 or 5, which will not make him win.

So, he should point at the section having angle
between 153° and 171°, to get a score of 14
points.

So, Statement I is definitely true according to
the question.

22. The score Sandy can get between angle 46° to
(b) 90° = 1, 18

and the score Sandy can get between angle
100° to 130° = 5, 12

So, the maximum score which Sandy can make
by aiming at these angle will be

          = 18 + 12 = 30

7 Measurement

1. Distance travelled by Ella starting from point A
(b)
$= AB + BC + CD + DE + EF + FA$
$= 20\,m + 20\,m + 15\,m + 9\,m + 7\,m + 10\,m$
$= 81\,m = 8100\,cm$ [$\because 1\,m = 100\,cm$]

2. Temperature shown in thermometer $= 41^\circ F$
(b)
So, temperature (in $^\circ C$) $= (41 - 32) \times \dfrac{5}{9}$

$$\left[\because {}^\circ C = ({}^\circ F - 32) \times \frac{5}{9}\right]$$

$= 9 \times \dfrac{5}{9} = 5^\circ C$

3. Given, length of each saree $= 8.28\,m$
(c)
Now, we will convert the metre in yards.
Now, $0.92\,m = 1\,yard$
$\therefore$ $1\,m = \dfrac{1}{0.92}\,yard$
$\Rightarrow$ $8.28\,m = \dfrac{8.28}{0.92}\,yards = 9\,yards$

So, measure of saree in yards is 9 yards.

4. Given,   1 square $= 5$ circles
(b)
So,   2 squares $= 10$ circles
and   1 triangle $= 4$ circles
So, weight of 2 squares + 1 triangle + 1 circle
$= (10 + 4 + 1)$ circles $= 15$ circles
Thus, 15 circles are required on the other side to balance the scale.

5. Temperature at which the cake is to be baked
(c)
$= 212^\circ F$
We know that, $^\circ C = ({}^\circ F - 32) \times \dfrac{5}{9}$
So, we have $(212 - 32) \times \dfrac{5}{9} = 180 \times \dfrac{5}{9} = 100\,^\circ C$

6. Here, 1 toy block $= 1$ cube of volume 1 cubic unit
(c)
$\therefore$ Number of toy blocks $=$ Volume of the stack
$= 3 \times 4 \times 3 = 36$

7. Distance between each plant $= 8\,cm$
(b)
Total length of boundary $= 12\,m$
$= 1200\,cm$ [$\because 1\,m = 100\,cm$]
So, number of plants which can be planted
$= \dfrac{1200}{8} + 1 = 150 + 1 = 151$

8. Amount of water in the glass $= 5\,mL$
(b)
Raise in height of water in glass after dropping the ball in it $= 8\,mL - 5\,mL = 3\,mL$
Now, $1\,mL = 1\,cm^3$
So, volume of ball $= 3\,cm^3$

9. Length of shirt bought by michelle
(c)
$= 58.5\,cm$
$\therefore$ Required length of shirt $= 58.5\,cm + 4 \times 2.5\,cm$
$58.5\,cm + 10\,cm = 68.5\,cm$ [$\because 1\,inch = 2.5\,cm$]

10. Temperature of vessel I $= 20^\circ C$
(c)
Temperature of vessel II $= 35^\circ C$
So, difference of temperatures of vessels
$= 35^\circ C - 20^\circ C = 15^\circ C$
Therefore, difference of temperature in fahrenheit
$= 15^\circ \times \dfrac{9}{5} + 32^\circ = 59^\circ F$ $\left[as\ {}^\circ F = {}^\circ C \times \dfrac{9}{5} + 32^\circ\right]$

11. Last year height of Jessy $= 1\,m\ 25\,cm$
(c)
Increase in height $= 12\,cm$
So, present height of Jessy
$= 1\,m\ 25\,cm + 12\,cm = 1\,m\ 37\,cm$
Height of Teresa $= 1\,m\ 8\,cm$
So, difference in the height of Jessy and Teresa $= 1\,m\ 37\,cm - 1\,m\ 8\,cm = 29\,cm$

12. Total weight of 2 pieces of gold
(d)
$= 6\,kg\ 755\,g + 5\,kg\ 550\,g$
$= 6.775\,kg + 5.550\,kg$ [$\because 1\,kg = 1000\,g$]
$= 12.325\,kg$
Weight of biscuit to be made $= 15\,kg$
So, weight of gold required
$= 15\,kg - 12.325\,kg$
$= 2.675\,kg = 2\,kg\ 675\,g$

13. Volume of box $1 = 2\,cm \times 3\,cm \times 4\,cm$
(b)
$= 24$ cubic cm
Volume of box $2 = 3.5\,cm \times 1.5\,cm \times 0.05\,m$
$= 3.5\,cm \times 1.5\,cm \times 5\,cm$ [$\because 1\,m = 100\,cm$]
$= 26.25$ cubic cm
So, volume of box 2 > volume of box 1.
Therefore, the height of water of vessel in which box 2 is dipped will raise more.

14. Weight of $\boxed{C}$ = 4 kg 800 g
(c)
$$= 4000\,g + 800\,g = 4800\,g$$
$$[\because 1\,kg = 1000\,g]$$
So, weight of $\boxed{A}$ = $\dfrac{4800}{3}$ = 1600 g $[\because 1\,C = 3A]$

∴ Weight of $\boxed{B}$ = $\dfrac{1600}{2}$ = 800 g $[\because 1\,A = 2B]$

15. Capacity of the locker
(b)
$$= Length \times Breadth \times Height$$
$$= 12\ inch \times 8\ inch \times 30\ inch$$
$$= 2880\ cubic\ inch$$
Volume of 1 book = 24 cubic inch
So, number of books which can be placed in the
locker = $\dfrac{Capacity\ of\ locker}{Volume\ of\ book}$ = $\dfrac{2880}{24}$ = 120

16. I. $°F = 0° \times \dfrac{9}{5} + 32 = 32°F$
(a)

II. $°F = 100° \times \dfrac{9}{5} + 32 = 212°F$

III. $°F = 35° \times \dfrac{9}{5} + 32 = 95°F$

IV. Difference $= 35°C - 25°C = 10°C$
Now, $°F = 10° \times \dfrac{9}{5} + 32 = 50°F$

17. Given,
(b)

 = 3 kg

⇒   3 = 3 kg

So,

1 = 1 kg

Now,

3 = 15

⇒   3 = 15 kg $[\because 1 \triangle = 1\,kg]$

1 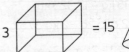 = $\dfrac{15}{3}$ = 5 kg

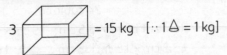

So,

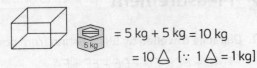 = 5 kg + 5 kg = 10 kg
$$= 10 \triangle \quad [\because 1 \triangle = 1\,kg]$$

So, 10 $\triangle$ are required to balance the scale.

18. Volume of bath tub (in cubic cm)
(a)
$$= 1.5\,m \times 0.7\,m \times 0.6\,m = 0.63\ cubic\ m$$
Now, $1\,m^3 = 1000\,L$
So, $0.63\,m^3 = 630\,L$
Now,
    Volume of bath tub = Capacity of 10 buckets
i.e. Capacity of 10 buckets = 630 L
So,   capacity of 1 bucket = $\dfrac{630}{10}$ = 63 L

19. Volume of cuboid shaped gold biscuits
(d)
$$= 30\,cm \times 20\,cm \times 0.05\,m$$
$$= 30\,cm \times 20\,cm \times 5\,cm \quad [\because 1\,m = 100\,cm]$$
$$= 3000\ cm^3$$
Volume of cube shaped brick
$$= 1.2 \times 1.2 \times 1.2\ m^3$$
$$= 1.728\ m^3$$
$$= 1728000\ cm^3$$
So, number of gold biscuits which can be
formed = $\dfrac{Volume\ of\ cube\ shaped\ brick}{Volume\ of\ cuboid\ shaped\ biscuits}$
$$= \dfrac{1728000}{3000} = 576$$

20. I. True,
(b)
    Total weight of candies = 3.6 kg + 0.75 kg
$$= 4.35\ kg$$
Weight of each box = $\dfrac{4.35}{5}$ kg = 0.87 kg

II. False,
    Vandy's height = $1\dfrac{3}{8}$ m = $\dfrac{11}{8}$ m

    Andy's height = $\dfrac{11}{8} + \dfrac{1}{4} = \dfrac{11+2}{8} = \dfrac{13}{8} = 1\dfrac{5}{8}$

III. False,
    weight of each can = $\dfrac{13338}{9}$ = 1482 L

IV. False, length of book is measured in metres or
    centimetre.

21. Total quantity of water that need to be put = 1 L
(c)
$$= 1000 \, mL \qquad [\because 1 \, L = 1000 \, mL]$$
Capacity of container 1 = 150 mL
Capacity of container 2 = 25 mL
Now, we have
Option (a), 150 mL × 4 + 25 mL × 6 = 600 + 150
$$= 750 \, mL$$
Option (b), 150 mL × 8 + 25 mL × 3 = 1200 + 75
$$= 1275 \, mL$$
Option (c), 150 mL × 6 + 25 mL × 4 = 900 + 100
$$= 1000 \, mL$$
So, option (c) will be correct combination.

22. Cost of 200 mL of cream = ₹ 400
(b)
Quantity of cream required = 1 L = 1000 mL
200 mL of cream is packed in 1 pot.
So, 1000 mL of cream will be packed in $\dfrac{1000}{200}$
$$= 5 \, pots$$
So, amount of money spent in buying 5 pots
$$= 5 \times 400 = ₹ 2000$$

23. Cost of 200 mL of condensed milk
(b)
$$= ₹ 250.50$$
Quantity of condensed milk required
$$= 500 \, mL$$
Quantity of condensed milk bought
$$= \dfrac{3}{5} \times 500 \, mL = 3 \times 100 = 300 \, mL$$
So, cost of condensed milk bought
$$= \dfrac{250.50}{200} \times 300 = ₹ 375.75$$

24. Volume of box 1 = 30 × 30 × 12 cubic ft
(a)
$$= 10800 \, cubic \, ft$$
Volume of box 2 = 20 × 20 × 12 cubic ft
$$= 4800 \, cubic \, ft$$
Volume of box 3 = 10 × 10 × 12 cubic ft
$$= 1200 \, cubic \, ft$$
So, total volume of three boxes
$$= 10800 + 4800 + 1200$$
$$= 16800 \, cubic \, ft$$
Number of small boxes = 140
∴ Volume of 1 small box
$$= \dfrac{\text{Total volume of 3 boxes}}{\text{Number of small boxes}}$$
$$= \dfrac{16800}{140} = 120 \, cubic \, ft$$

25. Quantity of lemon juice in 1 bottle = 1100 mL
(a)
Quantity of lemon juice in 2 such bottles
$$= 1100 \, mL \times 2 = 2200 \, mL$$
Now, amount of water in which 220 mL of lemon juice is mixed = 770 mL
So, amount of water in which 2200 mL of lemon juice is mixed $= \left[\dfrac{770}{220} \times 2200 \right] = 7700 \, mL$

∴ Total amount of lemonade made
$$= 2200 + 7700 \, mL$$
$$= 9900 \, mL$$
$$= 9000 \, mL + 900 \, mL$$
$$= 9 \, L \, 900 \, mL \qquad [\because 1 \, L = 1000 \, ml]$$

⑧ Pattern and Symmetry

1. As the ball is being rotated 180° clockwise, then
(b) in the next figure the ball will look like

2. Figure (b) is the correct other half of the given
(b) figure.

3. The given figure has 5 lines of symmetry
(d) passing through each of the vertex A, B, C, D and E as shown below :

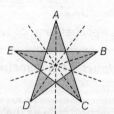

4. The lines of symmetry of each letter of the word
(b) are given below :

No line of   No line of   Horizontal line
symmetry   symmetry   of symmetry

So, 5 letters have a vertical line of symmetry.

5. On rotating half a turn the figures will become
(d) as follows

Figure (d) will look same on turning half a turn
as it is has rotational symmetry.

6. We have, figure as follows :
(a) A → non-symmetrical → ✓
     B → symmetrical → ✗
     C → symmetrical → ✗
     D → non-symmetrical → ✓

7. The given figure has following line of symmetry :
(d)

I.   II.   No line of
                 symmetry

III.   IV.   No line of
                 symmetry

Only Fig. III has vertical line of symmetry.
So, all the students were incorrect.

8. I. False, not all figure have line of symmetry.
(b)   e.g.

It is not symmetrical.

   II. False, some alphabets are not symmetrical.
       e.g. P, R, Q

   III. False, only letter O is symmetrical.

   IV. True

9. The series of picture follows the pattern :
(d) A A B C A A A B B C A A A A B B B C C
    So, option (d) is correct.

10. The number pattern is as follows :
(c)
$$7 + 7 \rightarrow 7 + 7 - 2 = 12$$
$$4 + 4 \rightarrow 4 + 4 - 2 = 6$$
$$3 + 3 \rightarrow 3 + 3 - 2 = 4$$
$$2 + 2 \rightarrow 2 + 2 - 2 = 2$$
So, $8 + 8 \rightarrow 8 + 8 - 2 = 14$

11. The pattern is that a square is added in each
(c) step first at right side, then at top, then at left
side and then at bottom.
So, the shape term will be

12. Joining
(c)

we get

13. The series of books is as follows :
(d)   3,   6,   12, ...
                 ×2   ×2

So, we have
1st 2nd 3rd 4th 5th 6th 7th 8th 9th 10th 11th 12th
and so on as follows :
   3,   6,   12, 24, 48, 96, 192, 384, ...

So, number of books on fifth rack is 48.

14. Given pattern of numbers is as follows :
(c) $1 = 0 \times 9 + 1$

         $11 = 1 \times 9 + 2$

       $111 = 1\,2 \times 9 + 3$

Also, $\overset{\frown}{1111} \rightarrow$ Four 1's $= 1\,2\,3 \times 9 + 4$

So, we have
     $1111111 \rightarrow$ seven 1's
∴ $\underline{1111111 = 123456 \times 9 + 7}$

15. Fig. (i) on being folded will form a cube as it has
(a) squares faces.
Fig. (ii) on being folded will form Fig. II i.e.
square pyramid. Fig. (iii) on being folded will
form cuboid as it has rectangular faces and
when folded Fig. (iv) will form a prism.
I. → (i) ; II. → (ii) ; III. → (iv); IV. → (iii)

16.
(b)

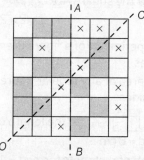

The number of squares having a cross sign should be shaded to make the given figure symmetrical about the line AB, which is obtained by folding the given figure along the line AB.

∴ Number of squares with cross sign = 9

17. We have the series as follows :
(c)
$1 + 2 + 3 + 4 + 5 + 6 + 7 + 8 + 9 + 10 = 55$

$11 + 12 + 13 + 14 + 15 + 16 + 17 + 18 + 19 + 20 = 155$

$41 + 42 + 43 + 44 + 45 + 46 + 47$
$\qquad\qquad + 48 + 49 + 50 = 455$

So, $91 + 92 + 93 + 94 + 95 + 96 + 97 + 98$
$\qquad\qquad + 99 + 100 = 955$

∴ $91 + 92 + 93 + 94 + 95 + 96 + 97$
$\qquad\qquad + 98 + 99 = 955 - 100$

18. The number series of the toffees is as follows :
(b)
$1\ \text{coin} \rightarrow 5$; $2\ \text{coins} \rightarrow 5 + 3 \rightarrow 8$

$3\ \text{coins} \rightarrow 8 + 3 \rightarrow 11$; $4\ \text{coins} \rightarrow 11 + 3 \rightarrow 14$

$5\ \text{coins} \rightarrow 14 + 3 \rightarrow 17$

$6\ \text{coins} \rightarrow 17 + 3 \rightarrow 20$

So, $7\ \text{coins} \rightarrow 20 + 3 \rightarrow 23$.

19. The figure of the given cards half turned is as
(c) follows :

So, only card I looks the same after taking $\dfrac{1}{2}$ turn.

20. Here, the series of figures depends on the last
(a) column of each figure which contains the following number of triangles :

I	II	III	IV
2	3	4	5

So, the total number of triangles used in the last and second last column of 17th pattern is

$18 + 17 = 35$

21. The series of items put in the boxes is as follows :
(d)

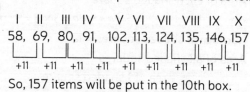

So, 157 items will be put in the 10th box.

22. According to the given pattern, we have
(c)

Figure	Number of triangles	Number of square
I	$4 \longleftarrow 1 \times 2 + 2$	1
II	$6 \longleftarrow 2 \times 2 + 2$	2
III	$8 \longleftarrow 3 \times 2 + 2$	3
IV	$10 \longleftarrow 4 \times 2 + 2$	4

So, the number of triangles in the 11th picture of the given pattern $= 11 \times 2 + 2 = 24$

⑨ Area and Perimeter

1. Since, perimeter of a figure is the sum of the
(c) length of its sides. So, length of the border is an example of perimeter.

2. Area of rectangle = Length × Breadth = 42
(d)
Option (a), $1 \times 26 = 26$
Option (b), $2 \times 13 = 26$
Option (c), $2 \times 21 = 42$ …(i)
Option (d), $6 \times 7 = 42$

So, options (a) and (b) are eliminated, because $26 \neq 42$.

and perimeter of rectangle = 26
$\qquad\qquad 2(l + b) = 26$
So, $\qquad\qquad l + b = 13$
From Eq. (i), we have $6 + 7 = 13$
∴ $\qquad\qquad l = 6$ and $b = 7$
So, option (d) is correct.

3. The figure can be labelled as shown below :
(c)

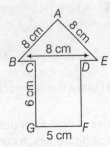

Perimeter of a figure
$$= \text{Sum of the length of its sides}$$
$$= AB + BC + CG + GF + FD + DE + EA$$
But $BC + DE = BE - CD = BE - GF \ [\because CD = GF]$
$$= 8\,cm - 5\,cm = 3\,cm$$
$\therefore$ Perimeter of figure $= 8 + 8 + 3 + 6 + 5 + 6$
$$= 36\,cm$$

4. Area of each shaded square
(a)
$$= \text{Side} \times \text{Side} = 3 \times 3 = 9\,cm^2$$
Number of shaded squares $= 12$
Area of all shaded squares
$$= \text{Area of 1 shaded square}$$
$$\times \text{Number of shaded squares}$$
$$= 9 \times 12 = 108\,cm^2$$

5.
(a)

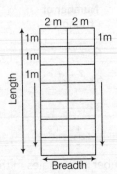

Given, the breadth of the space where one car is parked $= 2\,m$
The length of the space where one car is parked
$$= 1\,m$$
So, the length of the rectangular parking lot
$$= 1 \times 7 = 7\,m$$
[where, 7 is the number of rows of car spaces]
and   breadth $= 2 \times 2 = 4\,m$
[where, 2 is the number of columns of car spaces]
$\therefore$ Area of the parking lot $= 4 \times 7 = 28\,sq\,m$

6. Sides of the square $ABCD$
(b)
$$= \text{Length of the stick } ID - \text{Length of stick } DE$$
$$= 6\,m - 4\,m = 2\,m$$

$\therefore$ Area of the square $ABCD = \text{Side} \times \text{Side}$
$$= 2 \times 2 = 4\,m^2$$

7. I. False, perimeter of a figure is equal to sum of
(a)   its sides.

II. False, area of any regular figure is the product
of its sides.

III. True, ⎡4 cm 4 cm⎤ 4 cm , so the length of rectangle
formed $= 8\,cm$
Breadth of rectangle formed $= 4$
$\therefore$ Perimeter $= 2\,(l + b) = 2\,(8 + 4) = 2 \times 12 = 24\,cm$

IV. False
e.g. Let length of rectangle $= 3$ and breadth $= 2$
So, area of rectangle $= 3 \times 2 = 6$
Now, new length $= 6$ and new breadth $= 4$
$\therefore$ New area $= 6 \times 4 = 24$

V. True
Area of square $= \text{Area of rectangle}$
$$= 8 \times 2\,cm^2$$
$$= 16\,sq\,cm^2 = 4 \times 4$$
$\therefore$ Side of square $= 4\,cm$

8. The square will have the maximum area.
(b)
Maximum area for rectangle $= 26 \times 24 = 624\,m^2$
Maximum area for square $= 25 \times 25 = 625\,m^2$
Maximum area for $\frac{1}{2}$ rectangle $+ \frac{1}{2}$ square
$$= \frac{624}{2} + \frac{625}{2} = \frac{1249}{2} = 624.5\,m^2$$

9. We have,
(c)
(a) Perimeter $= 2\,(20 + 20) = 2\,(40) = 80\,m$
(b) Perimeter $= 2\,(40 + 10) = 2\,(50) = 100\,m$
(c) Perimeter
$$= 2\,(4000 + 0.1) = 2\,(4000.1) = 8000.2\,m$$
So, the must choose the land having boundary given in option (c).

10. The stair corner is as follows :
(b)

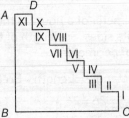

The perimeter of corner $ABCD$
$$= AB + BC + CD + DA$$

Corner CD = Length of sides

= I + II + III + IV + V + VI + VII + VIII + IX + X + XI

= 2.5 + 2.5 + 2.5 + 2.5 + 2.5 + 2.5 + 2.5

$\qquad$ + 2.5 + 2.5 + 2.5 + 2.5

= 11 × 2.5 = 27.5 cm

Length of side AB = Length of sides

= XI + IX + VII + V + III + I

= 6 × 2.5 = 15 cm

Length of side BC = Length of sides

= AD + X + VIII + VI + IV + II

= 6 × 2.5 cm = 15 cm

∴ Perimeter of corner $ABCD$

= 15 + 15 + 27.5 + 2.5 = 60 cm

11. Volume of one toy square block
(c)
$\quad$ = 1 cm × 1 cm × 1 cm = 1 cubic cm

Number of blocks in 1st step = 1

Number of blocks in 2nd step = 2

Number of blocks in 3rd step = 3 and so on.

Total number of blocks used to make a set having 10 such steps

= 1 + 2 + 3 + 4 + 5 + 6 + 7 + 8 + 9 + 10 = 55

So, volume of the staircase so formed having 10 such steps = 55 × 1 cubic cm = 55 cubic cm

12. I. Area = Length × Breadth
(b)
$\quad\quad\quad$ = 10 × 16 = 160 m²

II. Area = Side × Side

$\quad\quad\quad$ = 12 × 12 = 144 m²

III. ∵ $l = \dfrac{6}{5}b$

$\quad$ Also, $\quad 2(l + b) = 132$

$\Rightarrow \quad 2\left(\dfrac{6}{5}b + b\right) = 132 \Rightarrow \dfrac{11b}{5} = 66 \Rightarrow b = 30$

∴ $\quad\quad\quad l = 36$

∴ $\quad\quad$ Area = 30 × 36 = 1080 m²

IV. Perimeter = 2(20 + 16) = 2(36) = 72 m

13. We have,
(c)
$AG + AB + GF + BF$

$\quad$ = 8 + 8 + 8 + 8 = 32 cm

8 cm | X | C D | Y | G F E

A B, C D, Y, G F E (figure)

Now, the perimeter of figure is 40 cm.

∴ $\quad CD + FE = 40 - 32 = 8$ cm

and $\quad CD = FE = 4$ cm [since, Y is a square]

Hence, area of $Y = 4 × 4 = 16$ cm²

14. The bottom of the pens are rectangle.
(a)
So, perimeter of Jolly's dog's pen

$\quad = 2(l + b)$

$\quad = 2(8 + 12) = 2(20)$ $\quad\quad$ [∵ $l = 12$ cm, $b = 8$ cm]

$\quad = 40$ cm

Now, perimeter of Ted's dog's pen = 2(l + b)

$\quad = 2(6 + 15) = 2(21) = 42$ cm $\quad$ [∵ $l = 15$ cm, $b = 6$ cm]

Therefore, Ted will use more fencing to make the pen.

15.
(c)

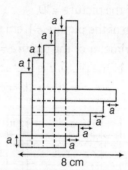

From the above figure, we see that length of each rectangle = $a + a + a + a = 4a$

Since, width of the figure = 8 cm

$\quad\quad 4a + 4a = 8$ cm $\Rightarrow a = 1$ cm

∴ Length of the figure = $4a + 5a = 9a$

$\quad\quad\quad\quad = 9$ $\quad\quad$ [∵ $a = 1$ cm]

So, perimeter of the figure = 8 + 9 + 8 + 9 = 34 cm

16. Length of the court = 50 ft
(b)
Breadth of the court = 30 ft

∴ Area of the court = $l × b = 50 × 30$

$\quad\quad\quad\quad = 1500$ sq ft

Paint required to cover 150 sq ft = 2 L

∴ Paint required to cover 1500 sq ft

$\quad = \dfrac{2}{150} × 1500 = 20$ L

$\quad\quad\quad\quad$ [by using unitary method]

17. Area of square sheet of poster board = $(l × b)$
(d)
$\quad\quad\quad = 12 × 12 = 144$ sq inch

Area of one invitation card = $l × b = 2 × 3$

$\quad\quad\quad\quad = 6$ sq inch

So, the number of cards that can be made

$= \dfrac{\text{Area of square sheet}}{\text{Area of card}} = \dfrac{144}{6} = 24$

18.
(c) Perimeter of square I $= 8\,cm = 4 \times$ Side

Area of square II $= 16\,cm^2 =$ Side $\times$ Side

So, side of square II $= 4\,cm$

$\therefore$ Perimeter of square II $= 4 \times$ Side $= 4 \times 4$

$= 16\,cm$

So, the length of wire $=$ Perimeter of square I

$+$ Perimeter of square II

$= 8\,cm + 16\,cm = 24\,cm$

19.
(d) Number of marks made on length of the picture $= 18$

So, length of the picture $= 19\,cm$

Similarly, number of marks made on the breadth of the picture $= 10$

$\therefore$ Breadth of the picture $= 11\,cm$

Hence, perimeter of the picture $= 2\,(l + b)$

[$\because$ the picture is rectangular in shape]

$= 2(19 + 11) = 2(30) = 60\,cm$

20.
(b)

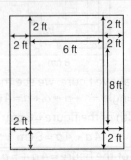

Length of the floor $= 8\,ft + 2\,ft + 2\,ft = 12\,ft$

Breadth of the floor $= 6\,ft + 2\,ft + 2\,ft = 10\,ft$

Area of the floor $= l \times b = 12 \times 10 = 120\,sq\,ft$

Area of carpet $= 6\,ft \times 8\,ft = 48\,sq\,ft$

[$\because$ length of carpet $= 6$ ft and breadth of carpet $= 8$ ft]

$\therefore$ Area of border

$=$ Area of floor $-$ Area of carpet

$= 120 - 48 = 72\,sq\,ft$

21.
(d) Size of a page of scrap book $= 7.5$ by $6\,cm$

Area of the page of the scrap book $= l \times b$

$= 7.5 \times 6 = 45\,cm^2$

Area of each stamp $= l \times b = 2.5 \times 1.5 = 3.75\,cm^2$

So, number of stamps in one page

$= \dfrac{\text{Area of page of the scrap book}}{\text{Area of one stamp}}$

$= \dfrac{45}{3.75} = 12$

$\therefore$ Number of stamps in 10 such pages

$= 12 \times 10 = 120$

22.
(a) Perimeter of Fig. I $=$ Sum of the lengths of sides

$= 5\,cm + 2\,cm + 2\,cm + 2\,cm + 2\,cm$

$+ 2\,cm + 5\,cm + 2\,cm + 2\,cm$

$+ 2\,cm + 2\,cm + 2\,cm = 30\,cm$

Perimeter of Fig. II $=$ Sum of the lengths of sides

$= 1\,cm + 3\,cm + 2\,cm + 2\,cm + 2\,cm$

$+ 1\,cm + 1\,cm + 3\,cm + 6\,cm + 3\,cm$

$= 24\,cm$

$\therefore$ Perimeter of Fig. I > Perimeter of Fig. II

So, Mihinaz needs to colour the boundary for Fig. I more with a black pen.

23.
(a) Area of classroom

$= l \times b = 18 \times 22\,sq\,ft = 396\,sq\,ft$

Space occupied by a bench $= l \times b$

$= 4 \times 2.5\,sq\,ft = 10\,sq\,ft$

Space occupied by 28 such benches

$= 10 \times 28 = 280\,sq\,ft$

Space occupied by almirah $= l \times b = 5 \times 4\,sq\,ft$

$= 20\,sq\,ft$

Space occupied by table $= l \times b = 3 \times 5\,sq\,ft$

$= 15\,sq\,ft$

So, space left $=$ Area of classroom

$-$ (Area of 28 benches $+$ Almirah $+$ table)

$= 396 - (280 + 20 + 15) = 81\,sq\,ft$

24.
(c) Total breadth of class III A, V and II

$=$ Length of assembly ground $= 6\,m$

So, breadth of each class $= 2\,m$ [$\because 6 \div 3 = 2$]

and length of each class $= 4\,m$

$\therefore$ Area of a class $= l \times b = 4 \times 2 = 8\,m^2$

So, area covered by 12 such classes

$= 12 \times 8 = 96\,m^2$

25.
(a) Area of assembly ground $= l \times b = 6 \times 3 = 18\,m^2$

So, area of hall $= \dfrac{2}{3} \times 18 = 12\,m^2$

Now, length of hall $=$ Length of three classes

$= 6\,m$

So, breadth of hall $=$ Area $\div$ Length

$= 12 \div 6 = 2\,m$

$\therefore$ Perimeter of hall $= 2(l + b) = 2(6 + 2)$

$= 16\,m^2$

10 Data Handling

1. Maximum number of books read (by Javed) = 15
(b) and minimum number of book read (by Tom) = 5

∴ Required difference = 15 − 5 = 10 books

2. Given, ▽ = 10, then 45 = 40 + 5
(c)
= 10 + 10 + 10 + 10 + 5

3. Total number of figures made = 25
(a) and total number of students = 50

So,

$$\text{👤} = \frac{\text{Total number of students}}{\text{Total number of figures made}} = \frac{50}{25} = 2 \text{ students}$$

4. Total number of muffins in the picture
(c)
= 21.5

and 1 muffin picture = 10 muffins

So, total number of muffins

Kristine baked in four days = 21.5 × 10 = 215

5. From the graph we can make the following table
(b)

Literature	Number of students in class V(A)	Number of students in class V(B)
Fantasy	9	4
Folktales	6	6
Science fiction	8	12
Sports	9	9

Thus, fantasy literature is more preferred in class V (A) than in class V (B).

The difference between the number of students who preferred fantasy in class V (A) than in class V (B) = 9 − 4 = 5

6. Number of orders completed in week 2
(d)
= 10 + 10 + 10 + 5 = 35   [∵ ▢ = 10, ▢ = 5]

So, number of orders completed in week 3

= 35 − 15 = 20

= ▢ ▢

7. Length of nail B = 7 ⊤
(c)
= 7 × 1.5

= 10.5 units

Length of nail D = 9 ⊤

= 9 × 1.5

= 13.5 units

∴ Required difference = 13.5 − 10.5 = 3 units

8. I. 25
(b)
↓ = 5

↓↓↓↓↓ = 5 × 5 = 25

II. 35

♠ = 70

$$\text{◢} = \frac{70}{2} = 35$$

III. 12 ☆ = 72

So, 1 ☆ = $\frac{72}{12}$ = 6

IV. 11

◇◇ = 24,

So, ◇ = $\frac{24}{2}$ = 12

∴ 11 ◇ = 11 × 12 = 132

Now, 132 = 11 ◇

9. Capacity of tank when completely filled with
(b) water = 120 litres

So, capacity of tank when half-filled with water
= 60 litres

∴ Time taken for the tank to be half-emptied
= 1 pm − 2:30 pm = 1.5 hours

10. The number of hours each child watch the TV is
(d) given below :

Mary	→	21
Peter	→	15
David	→	9
John	→	15
Susan	→	14
Mark	→	11
Clarie	→	22
Jane	→	12
Paul	→	18

So, Susan watched TV 14 hours a week.

11. Total of three maximum number of
(c) hours $= 22 + 21 + 18 = 61$ hours (from above question)

Total of three minimum number of hours the children have watched TV

$$= 9 + 11 + 12$$
$$= 32 \text{ hours}$$

∴ Required difference $= 61 - 32$ hours
$$= 29 \text{ hours}$$

12. We have by tally marks $\boxed{/}$ = 5
(a) Tally marks representing
super market $= \boxed{/}\ \boxed{/}\ \boxed{/}\ \sqsubset$

∴ Number of people who went to super market
$$= 5 + 5 + 5 + 2 = 17$$

13. Number of people who went to post office
(b)
$$= \boxed{/}\ \boxed{/}\ \boxed{/}\ \boxed{/}\ \square$$
$$= 5 + 5 + 5 + 5 + 4$$
$$= 24$$

Number of people who went to shoe shop
$$= \boxed{/}\ \boxed{/}\ \sqsubset$$
$$= 5 + 5 + 2$$
$$= 12$$

∴ Required difference $= 24 - 12 = 12$

14. Number of birthdays in each month.
(c)

Months	Number of birthdays	Months	Number of birthdays
January	2	November	0
February	1	December	2
March	6		
April	1		
May	7		
June	1		
July	3		
August	1		
September	2		
October	1		

So, only two months have number of birthdays more than 4 namely March (6) and May (7).

15. Number of children having birthdays coming
(c) after 31st January and before 1st July = Number of children having birthdays between 1st February and 30th June $= 1 + 6 + 1 + 7 + 1 = 16$

16. Temperature on Wednesday $= 27.5°C$
(d)
Temperature on Saturday $= 15°C$

∴ Difference $= 27.5°C - 15°C = 12.5°C$

17. Temperature on each day is as follows :
(a)

Sunday	→	12.5°C
Monday	→	17.5°C
Tuesday	→	22.5°C
Wednesday	→	27.5°C
Thursday	→	15°C
Friday	→	17.5°C
Saturday	→	15°C

Hence, on Tuesday the temperature was near 22.5°C which is between 27°C and 18°C.

18. The following table shows the number of sunny
(d) days and rainy days.

Months	Sunny days	Rainy days
January	14	$(31 - 14) = 17$
February	6	$(28 - 6) = 22$
March	16	$(31 - 16) = 15$
April	20	$(30 - 20) = 10$
May	18	$(31 - 18) = 13$
June	10	$(30 - 10) = 20$

So, month June had 20 rainy days.

19. Number of sunny days during the first three
(c) months are $= 14 + 6 + 16$

[from table in above question]

$$= 36$$

20. Month having highest number of rainy days
(c) = February (22). [from table in Q. No. 18]

21. Distance from E to $A = 50$ km
(c)
E to $B = 40$ km
E to $C = 20$ km
E to $D = 60$ km

So, option (c) shows the correct map.

22. Picture used to number of books read in August
(c)
$$= 11\frac{1}{2} \text{ } \square$$

If 1 $\square$ = 2 books,

so $11\frac{1}{2}$ $\square$ = 11.5 $\square$ = 11.5 × 2

$$= 23 \text{ books}$$

∴ Number of books read in August = 23

23. If 1 $\square$ = 4 books, then books read in June
(c)
$$= 10 \times 2$$
$$= 20 = 5 \times 4$$
$$(\square\square\square\square\square)$$
$$= 5 \square$$
[because, now $\square$ means 4 books]

24. The taxi driver made the most journeys on
(a) Tuesday (36).

So, total money collected on Tuesday
$$= 36 \times 112 = ₹4032$$

25. Number of journeys made on Monday = 23
(c)
Money collected on Monday
$$= 23 \times 85$$
$$= ₹ 1955$$

Number of journeys made on Wednesday = 18
Money collected on Wednesday
$$= 18 \times 69$$
$$= ₹ 1242$$

∴ Required difference = ₹1955 − ₹ 1242
$$= ₹ 713$$

Practice Set ①

1. Angle C is an obtuse angle as its measure is
(d) greater than 90°.

2. The pattern is as follows :
(b)
$$(14 + 7) \div 3 = 7$$
$$(17 + 8) \div 5 = 5$$
So, $(22 + 6) \div 7 = 4$

3. Number of cubes in top row = 5
(d)
Number of cubes in middle row
$$= 5 + 3 = 8$$
Number of cubes in last row
$$= 8 + 4 = 12$$
So, total number of cubes
$$= 5 + 8 + 12 = 25$$

4. Total number of pupils
(b)
$$= 50 + 120 + 90 + 20 = 280$$
Number of pupils who go by car = 90
So, the required fraction
$$= \frac{90}{280} = \frac{9}{28}$$

5.
(c)

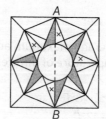

The places in the figure, which are crossed, are required to be shaded to make *AB* as its line of symmetry.

So, the number of triangles to be shaded to make *AB* as the line of symmetry is 4.

6. We have,
(c)
$$x + 2 \times 6 \div 3 = 52$$
∴ $x + 2 \times \dfrac{6}{3} = 52$
⇒ $x + 2 \times 2 = 52$
⇒ $x + 4 = 52$
∴ $x = 52 - 4$
$$= 48$$

7. Only the net of cube in option (d) will have no
(d) two faces having same alphabet meeting to form an edge.

8. Quantity of flour in bag $A = 15$ kg
(b) After pouring some quantity of flour in bag B from bag A, quantity of flour in bag $B = 8$ kg

So, remaining quantity of flour in bag
$$A = 8 + 3 = 11 \text{ kg}$$
∴ Quantity of weight transferred from bag A to bag $B = 15 - 11 = 4$ kg

9. Length of 1 blue ribbon $= 204$ cm
(d) Length of 5 blue ribbons $= 204 \times 5 = 1020$ cm

Total length of blue and yellow ribbons
$$= 22.84 \text{ m} = 2284 \text{ cm} \qquad [\because 1 \text{ m} = 100 \text{ cm}]$$
∴ Length of 8 yellow ribbons
$$= 2284 - 1020$$
$$= 1264 \text{ cm}$$

So, length of 1 yellow ribbon
$$= 1264 \div 8$$
$$= 158 \text{ cm}$$

10. Difference between average maximum and
(c) average minimum temperature of different cities are as follow :

New Delhi $= 38°C - 32°C = 6°C$

Kolkata $= 39°C - 27°C = 12°C$

Chennai $= 40°C - 28°C = 12°C$

Mumbai $= 32°C - 28°C = 4°C$

So, Mumbai had the least difference between its average maximum and average minimum temperature.

11. Length of 1 brick $= 0.2$ m $= 20$ cm
(a) $\qquad\qquad [\because 1 \text{ cm} = 100 \text{ cm}]$

Breadth of 1 brick $= 0.08$ m $= 8$ cm

Height of 1 brick $= 6$ cm

So, volume of 1 brick $= l \times b \times h$
$$= 20 \times 8 \times 6$$
$$= 960 \text{ cm}^3$$

Now, length of wall $= 10$ m $= 1000$ cm

Breadth of wall $= 0.06$ m $= 6$ cm

Height of wall $= 200$ cm

So, volume of wall $= 1000 \times 6 \times 200$
$$= 1200000 \text{ cm}^3$$
∴ Number of bricks $= \dfrac{1200000}{960} = 1250$

12. Greatest number of students that could be
(b) arranged in each row
$$= \text{HCF } (144, 128)$$
$$= 2 \times 2 \times 2 \times 2 = 16$$

13. Length of track I $= 8$ m
(b) and breadth of track I $= 6$ m

So, perimeter of track I $= 2(l + b)$
$$= 2(8 + 6)$$
$$= 2(14) = 28 \text{ m}$$

Length of track III
$$= (8 + 3 + 3 + 2 + 2) \text{ m}$$
$$= (8 + 6 + 4) \text{ m} = 18 \text{ m}$$
and breadth of track III
$$= 6 \text{ m} + 3 \text{ m} + 3 \text{ m} + 2 \text{ m} + 2 \text{ m}$$
$$= 6 \text{ m} + 6 \text{ m} + 4 \text{ m} = 16 \text{ m}$$

So, perimeter of track III $= 2(18 + 16)$
$$= 2(34) = 68 \text{ m}$$
∴ Difference of perimeters
$$= 68 \text{ m} - 28 \text{ m} = 40 \text{ m}$$

14.
(c)

$X \longmapsto\!\!\!\!\!\!\underset{Z \ 5/6}{\overset{23.9 \text{ km}}{\longrightarrow}} Y$

Fraction of journey completed $= \dfrac{5}{6}$

Fraction of journey left $= 1 - \dfrac{5}{6} = \dfrac{1}{6}$

So, total distance $= 23.9 \text{ km} \times 6 = 143.4$ km

Therefore, the distance between town X and town $Z = \dfrac{1}{2}(143.4) = 71.7$ km

15. Amount of money Jack had
(d) $= \dfrac{2}{5}$ amount of money Kerry had

Amount of money Jack had $+ 12.40 = \dfrac{3}{4}$

(amount of money Kerry had $- 12.40$)

So, $\dfrac{2}{5}$ amount of money Kerry had $+ 12.40$

$\qquad\qquad = \dfrac{3}{4}$ amount of money Kerry had $- 9.3$

$\Rightarrow \dfrac{3}{4}$ amount of Kerry had $- \dfrac{2}{5}$ amount of money

Kerry had $= 12.40 + 9.3$

$\Rightarrow \dfrac{7}{20}$ of money Kerry had $= 21.7$

So, money Kerry had $= \dfrac{21.7 \times 20}{7} = ₹\,62$

Practice Set ②

1. The pattern is as follows :
(b) The number in smaller square × 6
= The number in larger square

i.e. $36 \times 6 = 216$
$6 \times 6 = 36$

So, $D = 78 \times 6 = 468$
and $C = 78 \div 6 = 13$
∴ $C + D = 13 + 468 = 481$

2. We have, $P = 4595$
(c) So , $71099 - 4595 = 66504 = 67000$
[rounding off to nearest thousand]

3. Distance covered in one time = 2.5 mile
(c) So, total distance covered $= 3 \times 2.5$ mile
$= 7.5$ mile
Hence, option (c) is correct.

4. The length of bigger rectangle
(c) $= 14$ cm
Breadth of bigger rectangle = 6 cm
∴ Area of bigger rectangle
$= 14 \times 6 = 84$ cm²
Length of smaller rectangle
$= 14 - (8 + 2) = 4$ cm
Breadth of smaller rectangle
$= 6 - 4 = 2$ cm
∴ Area of smaller rectangle
$= 4 \times 2 = 8$ cm²
∴ Area of shaded part $= 84 - 8 = 76$ cm²

5. Given, [jug] − [glass] = 50 g
(b)
⇒ [glass] = [jug] − 50

[flask] − [jug] = 20 g

⇒ [flask] = 20 + [jug]

and [glass] + [jug] + [flask] = 240 g

∴ [jug] − 50 + [jug] + 20 + [jug] = 240

⇒ 3[jug] − 50 + 20 = 240

⇒ 3[jug] − 30 = 240

⇒ 3[jug] = 270

∴ [jug] = $\dfrac{270}{3}$ = 90

Now,

[flask] = 20 + 90
= 110 g

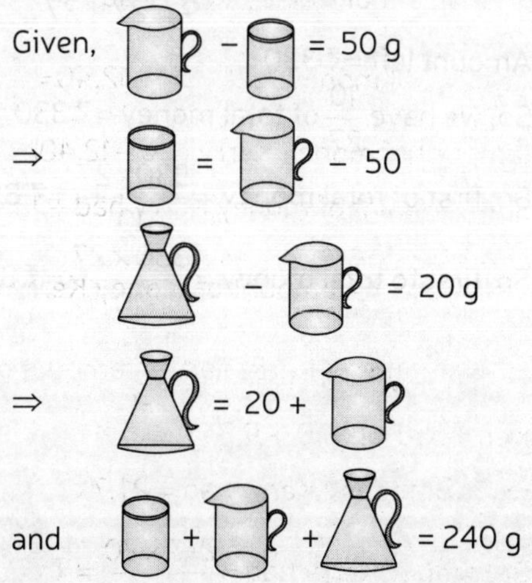

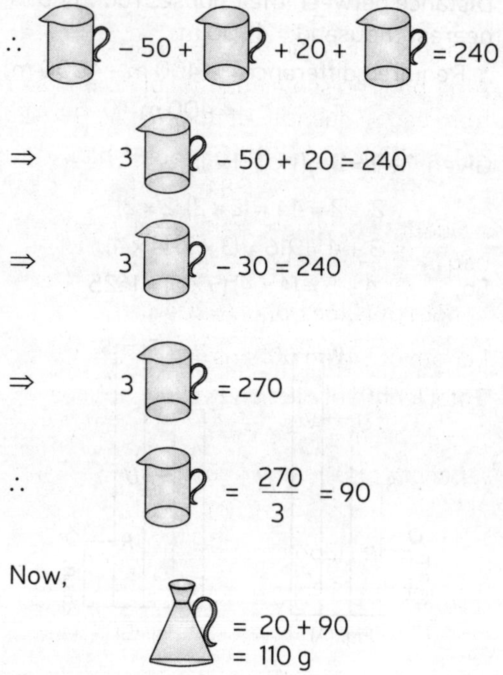

6. Volume of aquarium
(c) $= 3$ cm $\times 3$ cm $\times 3$ cm
$= 27$ cm³
Now, volume of one small cube
$= 1$ cm $\times 1$ cm $\times 1$ cm
$= 1$ cm³
So, number of small cubes that can be placed in the aquarium $= \dfrac{27}{1} = 27$
Now, number of cubes already placed
$= 1 + 3 + 6 = 10$
So, more number of cubes that can be placed in the aquarium $= 27 - 10 = 17$

7. According to the pattern,
(c)

19 = ▭ (with four rows of lines and four dots)

8. The shortest height at which the two stacks of
(b) boxes will be of the same height
= LCM of the heights of boxes
= LCM (12, 18)
= 36 inch

9. Distance between Andy's and Sam's house
(c) rounding to nearest hundred = 4400 m

Distance between their houses rounding to nearest thousand = 4000 m

∴ Required difference = 4400 m − 4000 m
= 400 m

10. Given, $1 + 1 = 11 = (1 \times 1)(1 \times 1)$
(c)
$$2 + 2 = 44 = (2 \times 2)(2 \times 2)$$
$$3 + 4 = 916 = (3 \times 3)(4 \times 4)$$
So, $\quad 4 + 5 = (4 \times 4)(5 \times 5) = 1625$

11.
(d)

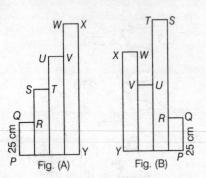

Fig. (A)　　Fig. (B)

Perimeter of figure $A = PQ + QR + RS + ST$
$$+ TU + UV + VW + WX + XY$$
$$= 25\,cm + 10\,cm + 25\,cm + 10cm$$
$$+ 25\,cm + 10\,cm + 25\,cm$$
$$+ 10\,cm + 100\,cm = 240\,cm$$

Perimeter of figure $B = PQ + QR + RS + ST + TU$
$$+ UV + VW + WX + XY$$
$$= 25\,cm + 10\,cm + 75\,cm + 10\,cm$$
$$+ 50\,cm + 10\,cm + 25\,cm$$
$$+ 10\,cm + 75\,cm = 290\,cm$$

So, difference in perimeters
$$= 290\,cm − 240\,cm = 50\,cm$$

12.
(b)

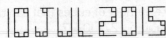

Number of right angles in letters = 6
Number of right angles in numbers = 16
∴ Required difference = 16 − 6 = 10

13.
(d)

1	2	3
4	5	6
7	8	9

$90° + 90° + 90° = 270°$

1	2	3
4	5	6
7	8	9

$90° + 45° = 135°$

Shimpy would have faced box 7, if turned 135° to the left.

14. Rainfall in July, 14 = 6.2 cm
(b) Rainfall in August, 13 = 1.8 cm
So, difference = 6.2 − 1.8 cm = 4.4 cm

15. Money used first $= \dfrac{4}{9}$ of total money
(a)
money left $= \left(1 - \dfrac{4}{9}\right)$ of total money
$$= \dfrac{5}{9} \text{ of total money}$$

Fraction of money used again
$$= \dfrac{1}{3} \times \dfrac{5}{9} = \dfrac{5}{27}$$
Fraction of money left $= \dfrac{5}{9} - \dfrac{5}{27} = \dfrac{10}{27}$

Amount left = ₹ 330
So, we have $\dfrac{10}{27}$ of total money = ₹ 330

So, first of total money $= \dfrac{330 \times 27}{10} = ₹ 891$

So, first to total money $= \dfrac{330 \times 27}{10} = ₹ 891$